Strategies for Modern Living

*A Commentary with the Text
of the Tannisho*

Strategies for Modern Living

A Commentary with the Text
of the Tannisho

By Alfred Bloom

With a Foreword by Yehan Numata

NUMATA CENTER
FOR BUDDHIST TRANSLATION AND RESEARCH
1992
Berkeley, California

First Printing, 1992
ISBN: 0-9625618-1-9
Library of Congress Catalog Card Number: 91-061704

Published by:
Numata Center for Buddhist Translation and Research
2620 Warring Street
Berkeley, California 94704

Printed in the United States of America

Contents

Foreword

      I have long desired to make available to the people in the West the *TANNISHO*, a Buddhist text expounding on the words of Shinran (A.D. 1173–1262), the founder of the popular Jodo Shin Sect. The book introduces Buddhism as a religion beyond good and evil.

      Several years ago the opportunity presented itself in the form of a commentary entitled *TANNISHO: A Resource for Modern Living* written by Dr. Alfred Bloom, currently Dean of the Institute of Buddhist Studies in Berkeley, California. This commentary is composed of radio talks given during the Moiliili Hongwanji Temple weekly broadcasts in Honolulu. Since I believe that this commentary accompanied by an English translation of the *Tannisho* would make an ideal publication, I asked the staff of the Numata Center for Buddhist Translation and Research to make an English translation and publish Dr. Bloom's commentary as a new book. I hope this book will make clear how the deep spiritual insights of the *Tannisho* can bring as much comfort to the troubled hearts of modern Westerners as they brought to troubled hearts in thirteenth century Japan. For as Shinran Shonin would be the first to tell us, times may change but human nature does not.

      I wish to express my deepest appreciation to: Moiliili Hongwanji Temple for sponsoring Dr. Bloom's radio talks on the *Tannisho*; Dr. Alfred Bloom for the permission to republish his work; the Buddhist Study Center in Honolulu, which first published the commentary; Ms. Ruth Tabrah, editor for the Buddhist Study Center, for her dedicated efforts to prepare the radio talks into book form; and the staff of the Numata Center for Translation and Research, Dr. Nobuo Haneda, the Reverend Seishin Yamashita, and the Reverend Shojo Oi, for the translation of the *Tannisho*, the preparation of the extensive glossary and index, and other editorial work.

It would give me great pleasure if this book would enable even one more person in the West to gain insight into the teachings beyond good and evil, and bring happiness and serenity into his or her life.

Yehan Numata
Founder, Buddhism Promoting Foundation

PART ONE

Tannisho: Notes Lamenting the Differences

by Yuien-bo

Preface

When I humbly reflect on the past and the present, I cannot help but deplore the fact that there now exist deviations from the true faith which was taught by our late master Shinran Shonin. I am afraid that this will cause confusion as the teachings are transmitted to future believers.

Unless we are fortunate enough to come into contact with a good teacher, how can we ever hope to enter the gate of Easy Practice? We must not distort the doctrine of Other Power with our own opinions and interpretations!

Thus, I am writing down some of the words of the late master Shinran Shonin which still ring in my ears. My sole purpose is to dispel the doubts of my fellow-believers.

I

When we believe that we have been saved by the inconceivable power of Amida's Vow and are therefore going to be reborn in the Pure Land, there arises from deep within us the desire to say the Nembutsu. At that moment we receive the benefit of being embraced by Amida Buddha, never to be cast away.

We should know that the Original Vow of Amida does not discriminate whether one is young or old, good or evil. True faith alone is necessary, for the Vow was made to save sentient beings who are burdened with great karmic evil and intense, fiery passions.

Thus, if we have true faith in Amida's Original Vow, other good acts are not necessary because there is no good superior to the Nembutsu. Neither should evil actions be feared, because no evil is capable of obstructing the working of Amida's Original Vow.

II

You have all travelled through more than ten provinces at the risk of your lives solely in order to see me and to ask me how to be born in the land of Utmost Bliss. But if you imagine that I know of ways to attain birth other than the Nembutsu, or that I know other teachings, you are greatly mistaken. If that is what you are looking for, you should visit the many distinguished scholars in Nara and on Mt. Hiei, who can answer in detail your questions on rebirth.

As for me, Shinran, I can only accept what my venerable master Honen said: "Just say the Nembutsu and be saved by Amida."

I, personally, do not know whether reciting the Nembutsu will be the seed of my birth in the Pure Land or whether it will create the karma which will cause me to fall into hell. But even if I discover that I have been misled by Honen Shonin, and that because I have said the Nembutsu I will fall into hell, I will have no regrets. If it were possible for me to become enlightened by performing some other practice, but I fell into hell because of saying the Nembutsu, I might well regret having been deceived. But since I am incapable of any religious practice whatsoever, hell will be my home in any case.

If Amida's Original Vow is true, Shakyamuni's teachings cannot be false. If the Buddha's teachings are true, Zendo's commentaries must not be false. If Zendo's commentaries are true, how can the words of Honen be deceptive? And if Honen's words are true, then what I, Shinran, say surely cannot be meaningless.

This is the faith of the foolish person that I am. And now, whether you entrust yourself to the Nembutsu or reject it is entirely up to you.

III

Even a good person can be born in the Pure Land, how much more so an evil person!

However, people commonly say, "Even an evil person can be born in the Pure Land, how much more so a good person!" This may sound reasonable, but it is contrary to the intent of Other Power, the power of the Original Vow. The reason for this is that those who believe that they themselves have the power to perform good acts are not inclined to rely completely on Other Power. Thus they are not in accord with the Original Vow of Amida. However, if they abandon their attachment to self-power and entrust themselves completely to Other Power, then they, too, will be born in the True Land of Recompense.

It was because of his compassion for those of us who are full of blind passions, and so are unable to escape from the bondage of birth and death through any religious practice whatsoever, that Amida made his Original Vow. And since his purpose was to enable people like us to attain Buddhahood, it is particularly the evil person who completely entrusts himself to Other Power who will be born in the Pure Land.

Thus the master said, "Even a good person can be born in the Pure Land, how much more so an evil person!"

IV

There is a real difference between the compassion of the path of the sages and the compassion of the Pure Land path.

In the path of the sages, compassion is expressed by feeling pity and sympathy for sentient beings and caring for them. But it is extremely difficult to help others escape the bonds of samsara as we would wish.

In the Pure Land path, compassion is expressed by saying the Nembutsu; quickly attaining Buddhahood through birth in the Pure Land; and then with a great compassionate and merciful heart, bestowing merits on all sentient beings to one's heart desire.

In this present life, it is hard to save others, no matter how much love and pity we feel towards them. Thus our compassion is limited and ephemeral. Only through saying the Nembutsu can perfect compassion be expressed.

V

I, Shinran, have not once said the Nembutsu for the sake of fulfilling my obligation of filial piety toward my late parents.

The reason is that all sentient beings have been my parents and my brothers and my sisters during my innumerable past lives. When I become a Buddha in the next life, I must save every one of them.

If the Nembutsu were a good act which we could perform by our own efforts, we could direct the merit that we acquire by saying it towards saving our parents. But since this is not the case, we should discard self-power and attain Buddhahood quickly. Then, through supernatural abilities and expedient means, we will be able to save all beings, beginning with those with whom we have past bonds, no matter what kind of karmic suffering they may be experiencing in the six realms of mortal existence and the four modes of birth.

VI

It is absurd for those who practice the Nembutsu exclusively to quarrel among themselves, saying, "These people are my disciples," or "These people are somebody else's disciples."

I, Shinran, have not even a single disciple. If I could bring people to say the Nembutsu, then I could call them "my disciples." But it would be preposterous to call somebody "my disciple" when he says the Nembutsu solely through the working of Amida's compassion.

If karmic conditions bring us together, we will come together. If karmic conditions separate us, we will part. Yet some say that if a person turns away from his teacher and follows another teacher, then even though he continues to say the Nembutsu, he will not be born in the Pure Land. This, too, is ridiculous. Are they saying that they can take back the true faith which was given by Amida as if it were their own? They should not speak this way.

When we are in accord with the principle of Naturalness and Spontaneity, we will feel grateful for the compassion of Amida Buddha and the compassion of our teachers.

VII

The follower of the Nembutsu treads the unobstructed Single Path. If we ask the reason why, it is because even the gods of heaven and earth reverence and bow to the devotee who has true faith, and the evil spirits and those of false ways never hinder. Sins and evil cannot result in karmic retribution. Because good deeds never surpass the Nembutsu, it is the unobstructed Single Path.

VIII

For the devotee, saying the Nembutsu is neither a religious practice nor a good act. It is not a religious practice because we do not perform it by our own deliberate effort. It is not a good act either because it is not something we do by our own deliberate effort. It is entirely the working of Other Power; it has nothing to do with self-power. Thus, for the devotee, it is neither a religious practice nor a good act.

IX

When I asked the master, "Even when I say the Nembutsu, I cannot really say that I feel like dancing for joy. And I find that I am in no hurry to get to the Pure Land. Why should this be so?", he answered, "I, Shinran, have also had this doubt. And now you, Yuien-bo, are feeling the same way!"

"When I think deeply about this, I conclude that it is precisely because I do not rejoice, when I ought to be dancing with joy, that I feel all the more assured of birth in the Pure Land.

It is our blind passions that keep us from rejoicing when we should rejoice. The Buddha, knowing that this would be so, said that we are all foolish beings filled with blind passions. That is how I know that Amida's compassionate Vow was made for people like us, and so feel all the more trust in it.

"If we are in no hurry to get to the Pure Land, if we worry that we might die whenever we are even slightly ill, that is also because of our blind passions and attachments. We find it difficult to leave this old home full of suffering in which we have been born again and again for incalculable ages. We do not long to be born in that Pure Land of peace where we have never been born before, so powerful are our burning passions. But no matter how reluctant we are to leave this world, when the karmic bonds which hold us to this realm of suffering wear out—when, in spite of everything we can do, our lives come to an end—we will go to the Pure Land. Amida has particular compassion on those who do not want to go there quickly. When I think of this, I feel all the more trust in Amida's great Vow and in his great compassion. And I feel that my birth in the Pure Land is certain.

"If I felt like dancing for joy and wanted to be born in the Pure Land right away, I might wonder whether it was really true that I am full of blind passions."

X

The master said, "The meaning of the Nembutsu is that it is beyond all logic. For it is beyond calculation, beyond explanation, and beyond understanding."

Special Preface

In the past, when Shinran Shonin was alive, fellow believers all shared the same faith and all had the same goal, namely, rebirth in the Land of Recompense in the life to come. They encouraged each other to travel all the way to the distant capital, where they all listened to Shinran's teachings at the same time. But recently, I hear that among the countless Nembutsu practitioners, young and old, who follow these direct disciples of Shinran, there are many who say things that are very different from anything Shinran ever said. I will now examine these groundless misconceptions in detail.

XI

Some people intimidate illiterate Nembutsu practitioners by asking, "Do you utter the Nembutsu because you believe in the inconceivable power of the Vow or because you believe in the inconceivable power of the Name?" They do not explain what they mean by these two "inconceivabilities." All in all, they confuse people.

This matter must be very carefully examined. It was through the inconceivable power of his Vow that Amida devised the Name which is easy to hold in mind and easy to say, and that he promised to embrace those who say this Name. Thus, it is all Amida's doing that we come to say the Nembutsu, and that we trust that the inconceivable power of his great compassionate Vow will enable us to escape from samsara. When we realize this, when we see that our own efforts had nothing at all to do with it, we are in accord with the Original Vow and will be born in the Pure Land. Therefore when we entrust ourselves to the inconceivable power of

9

the Vow, we are also entrusting ourselves to the inconceivable power of the Name. The inconceivable power of the Vow and the inconceivable power of the Name are one. There is no difference between them whatsoever.

Furthermore, those who think that good deeds can help them to be reborn in the Pure Land or that evil deeds can prevent it, strive to attain rebirth by their own efforts, believing that their own intelligence can save them. Such people turn the Nembutsu into a self-power practice. They do not entrust themselves to the inconceivable power of the Vow, nor to the inconceivable power of the Name, either.

But even those who do not trust in Amida will be reborn in the borderland, the land of sloth and pride, the castle of doubt, or the womb palace. Then, because of the Accomplishing Vow, they will eventually be reborn in the Pure Land. Such is the inconceivable power of the Name, which is nothing else but the inconceivable power of the Vow. Thus the Name and the Vow are one and the same.

XII

Some people say that those who do not read and study the scriptures are not assured of birth in the Pure Land. This idea is not even worth discussing.

All of the sacred texts which show us the truth of Other Power and explain its significance, state that if we entrust ourselves to the Original Vow and say the Nembutsu, we will become Buddhas. What else do we need to learn to be reborn in the Pure Land? Anyone who is confused about this teaching should by all means study, so that he may come to know the significance of the Original Vow. But people who read and study the scriptures and yet do not understand their fundamental meaning are truly pitiable.

Saying the Nembutsu is an easy practice, even for illiterate people who are quite ignorant of the scriptures. Those who follow the path of the sages consider learning to be of fundamental importance; hence their practice is difficult. And there is a passage in one of Shinran Shonin's letters about a man who engaged in study for the wrong reasons, studying just to gain fame and profit. It says, "I wonder if he will be born in the Pure Land in his next life."

Nowadays, people who do Nembutsu practice exclusively are engaging in doctrinal disputes with people who follow the path of the sages. While they argue, saying, "My school is superior; yours is inferior," enemies of the Dharma are appearing; and the Dharma is being slandered. But if we engage in doctrinal bickering, are we not slandering the Dharma ourselves?

Even if all of the other schools together should say, "The Nembutsu is only for worthless people. Its teachings are shallow and contemptible," we should not argue. We should simply reply, "We trust in what we are taught, which is that even foolish, illiterate people like ourselves, people of very inferior abilities, can be saved if we entrust ourselves to Amida. Highly gifted people may find this teaching beneath them; but for us, it is the highest teaching we can follow. Although other teachings may be superior, we are incapable of practicing them. Since the deepest desire of all the Buddhas is that everybody should be liberated from samsara, you should not hinder our practice." If we say this without showing any anger, who will harm us? Moreover, there is a sutra passage which says, "All sorts of blind passions arise during arguments. Wise people stay away from them."

Our late master said:

> Shakyamuni Buddha foretold that some would entrust themselves to this teaching but that others would denounce it. So, since I have entrusted myself to the Nembutsu while others are, indeed, denouncing it, I know that what the Buddha said was true, and am all the more certain that my birth in the Pure Land is assured. If it happened that some people believed in the Nembutsu but no one denounced it, one might wonder why.
>
> I am not saying that somebody has to vilify the Nembutsu. I am only saying that since the Buddha knew that some people would believe in it and some

would denounce it, he told us this fact in advance so that we would not be confused by it.

These days, it seems that people only study in order to silence their critics and overcome their opponents in debates and discussions. If, by studying, one becomes more and more aware of the true intent of the Buddha and the greatness of his compassionate Vow and if one is able to use such knowledge to explain, to those who are worried about how such wretched people as themselves could ever be reborn in the Pure Land, that the Original Vow is not concerned whether they are good or evil, pure or impure, then it is worthwhile to be a scholar. But if a scholar intimidates simple-hearted people who are saying the Nembutsu in accordance with the Original Vow by saying, "You should study!", he is a demon obstructing the Dharma, an enemy of the Buddha. Not only does he himself lack trust in Other Power, he confuses other people. He should not only tremble lest he go against his revered late master's teachings, but also grieve at not being in accord with Amida's Original Vow.

XIII

Some people say that those who are not afraid to do evil deeds because the inconceivable power of Amida's Original Vow will save them anyway are presuming on the Original Vow and therefore will not be reborn in the Pure Land. To say this betrays both a lack of trust in the Original Vow and a failure to understand how past karma causes both our good acts and our bad ones.

Good thoughts arise because of past karma. Evil thoughts and deeds are caused by past evil karma. The late Shonin said, "Know that all evil acts, even those as insignificant as a dust particle on the tip of the hair of a sheep or rabbit, are caused by past karma."

Once Shinran Shonin asked, "Yuien-bo, do you believe everything I tell you?"

"Yes, I do," I said.

Then he said, "If that is so, will you do anything I tell you to do?"

I humbly said yes.

"Would you murder a thousand people if it would guarantee your birth in the Pure Land?"

To this, I replied, "Even though you tell me to, I do not think I have it in me to kill even one person."

"Why, then, did you say you would obey me completely? Let this be a lesson. If you could just decide to do anything, then when I said, 'If you kill a thousand people, you will be reborn in the Pure Land', you would have gone out and started killing at once. But because your karma does not predispose you to kill even one person, you are not going to harm anybody. It is not that you do not kill because you are a good person. Likewise, it could happen that a person who does not want to hurt anybody could end up killing a hundred or a thousand people."

In saying this, the master showed us that when we think that the goodness within us makes us worthy of birth in the Pure Land and that the evil within us makes us unworthy of it, we are failing to grasp the fact that we can only be saved by the inconceivable power of Amida's Vow.

In Shinran Shonin's time, there was a man who held a mistaken view. He said that since the Vow exists to save people who do evil deeds, evil deeds must be the karmic cause of our rebirth in the Pure Land. Therefore, he reasoned, one should deliberately do evil things. When, eventually, Shinran heard of this man's misdeeds, he wrote a letter in which he said, "Do not take poison just because there is an antidote." He said this solely to dissuade this man from harboring this wrong view. He did not mean that evil actions can prevent one's birth in the Pure Land, not at all.

Shinran also said, "If we could not trust the Original Vow unless we kept the precepts and upheld the monastic rules, how could we ever escape from samsara?"

The truth is that when such wretched creatures as ourselves meet with the Original Vow, we always "presume" on it. But nonetheless, we will not do evil deeds unless our karma predisposes us to do them.

Shinran also said, "There is no difference between people who make their living by casting nets and fishing in the seas and rivers, or who hunt birds and wild animals in the plains and mountains; and people who engage in commerce or cultivate the fields and rice paddies."

He also said, "If our karma so moves us, we will do anything." Yet nowadays we see people playing the role of "aspirants for future Buddhahood," and acting as if only virtuous people should say the Nembutsu. These persons even post signs in training halls stating that persons who have done such-and-such impious things will not be admitted into the halls. Are they not just making an outward show of wisdom, goodness, and diligence while cherishing falsehood within?

Even those evil deeds which people do because they presume on the Vow have their roots in those people's past karma. We should simply leave both our good acts and our evil acts to our karma and entrust ourselves entirely to the Original Vow. That is the way of Other Power. In the *Essentials of Faith Alone*, it says, "Do you know the limits of Amida's power, that you think yourself too evil to save?"

It is precisely because we feel able to "presume on the Vow" that complete trust in Other Power grows firm in our hearts. If you got rid of all your evil karma and blind passions before entrusting yourself to the Original Vow, then, fine, you would never think of presuming on the Vow. But if you got rid of all your blind passions, you would become a Buddha then and there. And for a Buddha, the Vow that Amida made after five kalpas of contemplation would not be necessary.

People who admonish others against presuming on the Vow seem to be full of blind passions and defilements themselves. So are they not themselves presuming on the Vow? What kind of evil act is "presuming on the Vow" and what kind isn't? Is not such talk a product of immature thinking?

XIV

Some people believe that one utterance of the Nembutsu wipes away all of the evil karma that one has accumulated over eight billion kalpas.

The basis for this assertion is a passage in a sutra about an evildoer who is guilty of the ten evil deeds, has committed the five deadly sins, and has never said the Nembutsu in his life. But, through the guidance of a good teacher, he begins to say it on his deathbed. By saying it once, he wipes away the evil karma that he has accumulated over eight billion kalpas. By saying it ten times, he eradicates the evil karma that he has accumulated over eighty billion kalpas, and so is reborn in the Pure Land.

The sutra mentions "one utterance" and "ten utterances" in order to impress upon us the seriousness of the ten evil deeds and the five deadly sins, and to show us how the Nembutsu takes all of our evil karma away. But all this falls far short of what we believe. The reason is as soon as Amida's light shines upon us and awakens in us an instant of complete trust in his great Vow, we are endowed with indestructible diamond-like faith. From that moment on, we are assured of being reborn in the Pure Land. And when our lives come to an end, all of our blind passions, all of the evil within us, are transformed into the wisdom of perfect enlightenment; and we are awakened to the truth of non-origination.

We should look on the Nembutsu as an expression of gratitude for the Buddha's great benevolence and compassion. We should say it all our lives, thinking, "If it were not for Amida's compassionate Vow, how could such a wretched evil-doer as myself ever hope to be liberated from samsara?" If we believe that we are extinguishing our evil karma every time we say the Nembutsu, we are trying to eliminate that karma and attempting to attain rebirth in the Pure Land by our own efforts.

If we believe that every single thought that we have in a lifetime is another fetter binding us to the endless round of birth and death, then we can only be reborn in the Pure Land by saying the Nembutsu up until the very end of our lives. But it may be our karma to die in some totally unforeseen accident, or to die of some extremely painful disease. If that happens, it will be difficult to remain in the right state of mind and difficult to say the Nembutsu. So how could we nullify the evil effects of karma that we accumulate just before death? And if we could not nullify the effects of evil karma, how could we be reborn in the Pure Land?

If we entrust ourselves to the Vow which embraces and never casts away, then if we die suddenly and unexpectedly even after committing evil acts, or die without saying the Nembutsu, we will immediately be reborn in the Pure Land. Moreover, even if we are able to say the Nembutsu at the end of our lives, we are expressing gratitude for Amida's compassion, entrusting ourselves to Amida all the more as the time of our enlightenment draws nearer.

People who pray to be in the right state of mind at the end of their lives are trying to eradicate their evil karma by themselves. This shows that they have a self-power mentality and that they have no real trust in Other Power.

XV

Some people claim to have attained Buddhahood in this very body, full of blind passions though it is. This claim is preposterous.

The attainment of Buddhahood in this very body, that is, liberation through the three mystic practices, is the goal of Shingon esotericism. And the One Vehicle teaching expounded in the *Lotus Sutra* advocates purification of the six sense organs through "the four practices for the attainment of happiness." These difficult practices, which lead to the attainment of enlightenment through meditation, can be performed only by people of superior ability.

By contrast, the goal of the Other Power teaching of Pure Land Buddhism, attained through absolute trust in the Original Vow, is enlightenment in one's next life. This path is easy to practice and therefore suitable for those of inferior ability. It does not discriminate between good people and evil people.

It is extremely difficult to eliminate our blind passions and to sever our evil karma in this life. It is so difficult that even the holy monks of the Shingon and Tendai schools pray for enlightenment in the life to come. So what is to be said about people like us?

It does not matter that we lack wisdom and cannot observe the precepts. If we board the ship of Amida's Vow, we, too, will cross the sea of suffering, the dreadful ocean of birth and death. And as soon as we reach the shores of the Pure Land, the dark clouds of passions will clear away and we will see the bright moon of things-as-they-really-are. At that moment we will become one with Amida's unhindered light and will radiate blessings on all sentient beings throughout the ten quarters. Then and only then can we say that we have attained enlightenment.

Are those who claim to have attained enlightenment in this very body able to manifest themselves in various Transformed Bodies, as a Buddha should be able to do? Do they have the thirty-two major marks and the eighty secondary features of a Buddha? Can they teach the Dharma and save sentient beings as Shakyamuni did? That is how we would recognize a Buddha who had attained enlightenment in this life.

Shinran wrote in a *wasan*:

> At the moment when unshakable, diamond-like trust
>   in the Original Vow
> Takes root within us,
> We are embraced by the light of Amida's compassion
> And escape samsara forever.

This means that at the moment when absolute trust in Amida takes root in our hearts, we are embraced never to be abandoned. After that we no longer wander in the endless cycle of birth and death. That is why Shinran Shonin wrote that we "escape samsara forever." To confuse this with enlightenment is truly a pathetic misunderstanding!

The late Shonin said, "In the Jodo Shinshu, we entrust ourselves to the Original Vow in this life and then attain enlightenment in the Pure Land. That is what I was taught."

XVI

Some people say that whenever a Nembutsu practitioner becomes angry, does something wrong, or has an argument with a fellow practitioner, he should repent and try to have a change of heart. This reflects an attitude that we should seek rebirth in the Pure Land by refraining from evil and doing good.

A person who says the Nembutsu wholeheartedly and exclusively experiences only one great change of heart. This happens when a person who has never before grasped the true significance of Other Power of the Original Vow is inspired by Amida's wisdom and realizes that he, an ordinary person with an ordinary mind, cannot possibly attain rebirth in the Pure Land. He therefore casts off all his old ways of thinking and entrusts himself entirely to the Original Vow. This is what is called "the change of heart."

If we could not attain birth in the Pure Land without going through a change of heart every time we did something we should not do, we would have to go through changes of heart night and day. Would that not make a mockery of Amida's Vow to "embrace us and never cast us away"? For our lives can end between the time that we exhale and the time that we inhale again. What if we were to die without going through a final change of heart or without thinking gentle and patient thoughts?

Some people claim that they trust in the power of the Vow but think in their hearts that although the Vow is said to have inconceivable power to save evil people, it is, after all, mainly designed to save good people. Thus they doubt the power of the Vow and do not really trust in Other Power. They will be reborn in the borderland—how sad!

Once genuine trust in the Original Vow takes root in our hearts, Amida will bring about our rebirth in the Pure Land.

We must give up all of our own efforts for our rebirth. Even if we are evil, our hearts will naturally grow more gentle and patient by relying on the power of the Original Vow ever more. We should not harbor clever thoughts about how we are going to manage to be reborn into the Pure Land. Instead, no matter what happens, we should, with the warmest gratitude and devotion, constantly remind ourselves of the depth of Amida's compassion. Then we will find ourselves saying the Nembutsu effortlessly. This is Naturalness and Spontaneity. If we truly discard all of our own efforts and contrivances, what remains is Naturalness and Spontaneity. It is purely and simply Other Power.

Yet I have heard that some people say, with a knowing air, that "Naturalness and Spontaneity" has another meaning. This is deplorable.

XVII

Some people say that those who are reborn in the borderland will eventually fall into hell. Where in the scriptures is there a passage that says this? It is deplorable that people who call themselves scholars say such things. How are they reading the sutras, commentaries, and Buddhist scriptures?

Shinran Shonin taught me that practitioners who do not truly trust in Amida, who doubt the Original Vow, will be born in the borderland. Then, after they expiate their sin of doubting the Vow, they will attain enlightenment in the Land of Recompense.

Since few practitioners have true faith, Amida will lead many into the borderland. To say that in the end they are born there in vain [i.e., fall into hell] is to say that the Buddha has deceived us.

XVIII

Some people claim that the size of one's offerings determines whether one will become a large Buddha or a small Buddha.

This statement leaves me speechless. It is utter nonsense.

To begin with, how could anyone determine the size of a Buddha? When the size of a great Dharma teacher [i.e., Amida Buddha] in the Pure Land is described in a sutra, reference is being made to his Body of Recompense. A Buddha who has awakened to things-as-they-really-are transcends all categorization. He has neither shape, long or short, square or round, nor color, blue, yellow, red, white, or black. How, then, is it possible to tell whether the Buddha is large or small?

There is a sutra passage which states that by saying the Nembutsu, one may have a vision of a transformed Buddha. It also says that if you say the Nembutsu loudly, you will see a large Buddha; and if you say it softly, you will see a small Buddha. Perhaps some people have interpreted this passage in a distorted way so as to make it apply to offerings.

Of course it may be said that those who give offerings are practicing the *paramita* of giving. But though you offer great treasures to the Buddha and precious gifts to your teacher, if you do not have true faith, it is pointless. And even though you may not give a single sheet of paper or a single half *sen* for the Buddha Dharma, you are in accord with Amida's Vow if you surrender yourself to Other Power in deep faith.

It seems that some people are just using the Buddha Dharma to intimidate their fellow-practitioners into satisfying their greed.

Epilogue

1

All of the problems that I have discussed arise because believers differ in their understanding of faith.

According to the late Shinran Shonin, very few of Honen Shonin's many disciples had the same faith as their master. Thus Shinran got into an argument with his fellow practitioners when he said, "Zenshin's [i.e., My] faith and Honen Shonin's faith are one."

Seikan-bo, Nembutsu-bo, and other fellow disciples strongly objected, saying, "How can you have the same faith as Honen Shonin?"

Shinran replied, "If I said that I had Honen Shonin's great wisdom and learning, that would, indeed, be absurd. But as for my faith that I will be reborn in the Pure Land, mine does not differ from his at all. His faith and mine are one."

But the others still argued, "How can that be?" Finally they told Honen Shonin all about the argument and asked him to decide who was right and who was wrong. At this Honen declared, "My faith is a gift from Amida Buddha. Shinran's faith, too, is a gift from Amida Buddha. Therefore his faith and mine are one. Those with a different kind of faith will not go to the Pure Land where I, Honen, am going."

If this could happen in Honen's day, it seems likely that some of the people who practice the Nembutsu exclusively today do not have the same faith as Shinran's.

2

Although my words must seem repetitious, I have written them down anyway. For while life still clings to this old body like a dewdrop to a withered blade of grass, I will be able to listen to the questions of those around me and tell them what Shinran Shonin taught. But I am afraid that there will be confusion among my fellow-believers after these eyes are closed.

Whenever advocates of the mistaken views which I have discussed try to mislead you, you should carefully read those sacred writings which the late Shonin most approved and which he himself used to read. In Buddhist scriptures, true and real teachings are generally intermixed with expedient and temporary ones. The Shonin intended that we should abandon the expedient and keep the real, set aside the temporary and follow the true. You must be very careful not to misread the sacred scriptures. I have selected some important passages and appended them to this book as a standard reference.

21

3

Shinran Shonin often said, "When I deeply consider the Vow which Amida made after five kalpas of contemplation, I realize that it was made for me, Shinran, alone! Therefore I am filled with gratitude for the Original Vow, with which Amida decided to save me, burdened with evil karma though I am."

As I contemplate these words now, I think that they are not at all different from Zendo's golden statement, "Know that we are in reality foolish beings weighed down with evil karma, who have been drowning in samsara for immeasurable kalpas, who wander through an endless cycle of birth and death with no chance of liberation whatsoever."

Thus, by giving himself as an example, Shinran showed us how deluded we are—how we know neither the depths of our own karmic evil nor the greatness of Amida's compassion. How grateful I am to Shinran!

I and other people only talk about what is good and what is bad. We do not pay any attention to Amida's compassion. But the late Shonin used to say, "I know nothing at all about good and evil. If I possessed Amida's ability to tell whether something is good, then I would know what 'good' is. And if I possessed Amida's ability to tell whether something is evil, then I would know what 'evil' is. But for a foolish being full of evil passions, living in this burning house, this world of transiency, all things are deceptive, vain, and unreal. The only truth is the Nembutsu."

Indeed, we speak only empty things to each other. In that connection, there is one thing I find really lamentable. That is that when we discuss among ourselves the nature of faith and its relationship to saying the Nembutsu, or when we explain these things to others, some people, just to win an argument or to silence other people, claim that Shinran said things that he never said. How shameful and deplorable! We should stop and think about this!

Although the words I am writing are by no means my own, I am afraid that they must sound foolish. After all, I do not know the sutras and commentaries and am incapable of grasping the profound doctrines of Buddhism. Nonetheless, recalling only a hundredth part of what the late Shinran said, I am writing it down.

How sad it is when someone who has been fortunate enough to say the Nembutsu is reborn in the borderland instead of being reborn in the Pure Land right away! Therefore, with tears in my eyes, I wet my brush and write all this down so that there may be no differences in faith among believers of our tradition.

This text is to be called the *Tannisho (Notes Lamenting the Differences)*. It should not be shown openly.

PART TWO

Strategies for Modern Living: A Commentary on the *Tannisho*

by Alfred Bloom

CHAPTER 1

Why the *Tannisho* Was Written

The *Tannisho*, the succinct religious classic of Shin Buddhism, offers rich resources to modern men and women struggling with the contemporary problems of human conflict, competition, and confusion.

In radio programs, on the television screen, in our personal environments of work, community activities, and friendship, we encounter many analyses and criticisms of the modern technological developments which have, in a very real sense, enslaved and impoverished so many of us. We know the symptoms of our condition only too well.

We are succumbing to the glamour of our own material inventions. Our lives are often empty despite our material gains. The dilemma of the usual criticism, analysis, lamentation, and warning as to our desperate alienation, our frustrations and anxiety and deep loneliness is that only our symptoms are analyzed and our problems are intimately described, but no solution provided. In fact, contemporary critics seldom seem to see the real problem that lies behind our symptoms, or to recognize that though in the modern era technology has flowered, the roots of mankind's problems remain unchanged despite the external changes of progress and civilization. What strikes us in our times is not the uniqueness of our problems, but the inescapable visibility of symptoms of the old, basic problems emerging in our feelings of anxiety, alienation, loneliness, and in global and personal conflict.

In ancient times, men used clubs, spears, and bows and arrows to kill each other. Today we use guns and bombs. Yet, improvements in technology, the greater efficiency and wider scope in killing, do not alter the basic human fact that whatever the tools or implements, people are just as killed. And the problems that result in this killing are with us as pervasively as they were in the first days of man's recorded history. Human conflict, competition, and confusion beset us now as they did our ancestors.

Three thousand years ago in India, sages described our problems as all being rooted in the problem of the ego, the problem of desires, and the problem of human passions. Since the time of the Buddha, it has been recognized that, for the most part, each human being's passions are relatively the same. The only superficial, visible difference is that some may have more opportunity to employ their passions in the service of their self-interest. The sages who followed the teachings of the Buddha, and over the centuries further developed and expounded those teachings, tried to understand how the ego and the passions function within us, what it was that would stimulate them, in the hope that we could bring them under control.

On the political level, our passions are restrained through the pleasure-pain principle. Since we like pleasure more than pain, we will obey the law, because of some pain or restriction we incur if we do not. In discussions of capital punishment, we talk much about the value of the practice of capital punishment as a deterrent. Buddhism early recognized that simply deterring or repressing passions or desires did not remove them. Rather, the sages understood that in driving passions deeper into the self, they would emerge in more subtle and dangerous ways. Paradoxically, one of these ways is in religion, which may itself become a field for the expansion of ego-aggression and self-centered desires. Such may well have been the tragic case of the Jonestown Peoples' Temple mass suicides late in 1978 in Guyana.

Eight hundred years ago, in the medieval Kamakura period (1185–1332) in Japan, one of the most important thinkers who perceived the subtle nature of the ego masquerading under the cloak of piety and spirituality was Shinran Shonin (1173–1262), the son of a once noble family whose fortunes had diminished as they fell from political favor. Consequently, at the age of nine, Shinran went to become a monk on Mt. Hiei, then the center of Japan's contemplative and scholastic Buddhism. Because of the disruption and political turmoil that had affected his family and himself, Shinran had reason even at so early an age to begin to contemplate the real nature of the human condition.

For the next twenty years he assiduously practiced many disciplines, and rigorously followed the Buddhist regulations of the monastery. At age twenty-nine, it seemed to him he had failed in his years of sincere and earnest effort. His discipline, his resolve, gave him no assurance that he would ultimately achieve enlightenment and emancipation from finite mortal bondage. He became anxious about his future destiny, and we know from his various writings that his feelings were so intense that he walked down off Mt. Hiei and entered a period of meditation in the Rokkakudo in Kyoto. There, after almost one hundred days of seclusion, he received the spiritual impulse to visit Honen Shonin, who was proclaiming the sole practice of Nembutsu—the recitation of Amida's Name—as the way of salvation.

When he reached Honen, and became his disciple, Shinran felt that his spiritual destiny was secure. Nevertheless, the master and disciple separated, never to meet again, when Honen's Pure Land teachings fell under the persecution of the government. All were banished from Kyoto. Shinran was exiled to Echigo and then moved to the eastern plain, the Kanto region. His life and his description of himself were "neither priest nor layman." He married; fathered a family of six children; and, on the uncertain income of a religious teacher, began to understand the realities of human existence which he had not known as a monk. He lived in intimate association with the peasants of that region, one with them in their struggles in everyday life. Viewed through the realities of this experience, religion assumed a new meaning for him. Out of his spiritual struggle, out of his existential setting, out of his contemplation, and out of the inspiration he received from his years of intense study of previous Buddhist teachers, came Shinran's significant reinterpretation and understanding of Buddhism and, indeed, of religion as a whole.

Although in his later years, after his return to Kyoto, Shinran's many writings seem to be complicated and difficult, his was a popular teaching. He considered that he was teaching for the unlettered person, the person who could neither read nor write, and that what he was presenting to them was both universal and simple. "Simple" teaching does not here mean "simplistic." Shinran's thought had a profound basis, but that profound basis did not require his followers to know in detail all the subtleties and philosophical distinctions ordinarily required in order to explain and defend a religious teaching. There was scholarly depth if one wished to pursue it; but it was a depth that explained in Buddhistic and scholarly terms a faith that could also be experienced by the single-hearted practice of listening to the teachings; taking them into one's life; and, when conditions were ripe, yielding oneself spontaneously to the embrace of Amida's Vow-Power. Shinran's teachings thus had a wide appeal. From his virtually unknown and obscure background as a thinker of the thirteenth century, Shin Buddhism—the sect that follows his teachings—became one of the largest Buddhist movements in Japan and perhaps in the world. In this twentieth century, it has spread to America and Europe.

After Shinran's death, the institutionalization of his teachings gave rise to the development of numerous problems. Since they had a certain subtlety and paradoxical nature, they could be misunderstood, and they were. From Shinran's writings, we can see that there was conflict about his teachings even in his own lifetime. He was not authoritarian or punitive. He does not condemn those whom he thought were in error. But after he died, the problems continued and were compounded. One of his followers, Yuien-bo, a man of whom we know little, became so concerned for the future of the movement that he wrote the *Tannisho*—"Notes Lamenting the Differences." In this slim volume Yuien-bo expressed his sorrow that the community of fellow-believers could not be more united and clear in their understanding of the essentials of Shinran's teaching. The first section of his book gives pithy, gem-like quotations from Shinran. The second section is a more lengthy discussion of the implications of Shinran's teaching as applied to specific problems that were then afflicting the Shinshu community.

The *Tannisho* contains a wealth of human, spiritual insight. It brings out Shinran's understanding of Buddhism and the nature of religion in a way that remains relevant to our own times. It is my personal feeling that Shinran Shonin was a man who was not only far ahead of his own time, but even runs in front of ours. We have yet to appreciate the breadth and depth of his spirit. It is a wondrous thing that the *Tannisho*, so small a book that it may be read completely in perhaps fifteen to twenty minutes, brings together in concentrated form all the essential elements of Shinran's understanding. This understanding is confirmed by the voluminous writings of Shinran himself, which are more expansive and detailed and, hence, more difficult for ordinary people.

The *Tannisho* is written in most simple language. Its text is regarded as a literary as well as a religious classic in Japan. The simplicity of its expression, the power of its thought, has been translated in several English versions but none yet approach the lyricism of the original Japanese. However, the essence of Shinran's teachings leaps through the barricades of translation, as can be seen in chapter one:

> When we believe that we have been saved by the inconceivable power of Amida's Vow and are therefore going to be reborn in the Pure Land, there rises from deep within us the desire to say the Nembutsu. At that moment we receive the benefit of being embraced by Amida Buddha, never to be cast away.

31

We should know that the Original Vow of Amida does not discriminate whether one is young or old, good or evil. True faith alone is necessary, for the Vow was made to save sentient beings who are burdened with great karmic evil and intense passions.

Thus, if we have true faith in Amida's Original Vow, other good acts are not necessary because there is no good superior to the Nembutsu. Neither should evil actions be feared, because no evil is capable of obstructing the working of Amida's Original Vow.

CHAPTER **2**

About Yuien-bo

All we know about the *Tannisho*'s author, Yuien-bo,[1] is that he was an intimate friend and follower of Shinran. He must have possessed a remarkable spiritual sensitivity in selecting the materials he felt represented Shinran's deepest thought.

In the preface to the *Tannisho*, Yuien-bo indicates his motivation for writing. He has observed the disunity and conflict that have arisen in the Shinshu community and desires to clarify the issues in order to preserve the faith. Thus his text is called *Notes Lamenting the Differences*. In order to resolve these, he gathered together the words of Shinran as a guide in considering these differing points of view. He explains:

> When I humbly reflect on the past and the present, I cannot help but deplore the fact that there now exist deviations from the true faith which was taught by our late master Shinran Shonin. I am afraid that this will cause confusion as the teachings are transmitted to future believers.
>
> Unless we are fortunate enough to come into contact with a good teacher, how can we ever hope to enter the gate of Easy Practice? We must not distort the doctrine of Other Power with our own opinions and interpretations!

Thus, I am writing down some of the words of the late master Shinran Shonin which still ring in my ears. My sole purpose is to dispel the doubts of my fellow-believers.

This short paragraph is the entire preface—only a few lines and yet it gives insight into the nature of tradition and the problems of disagreement within a religious community. Yuien-bo had observed events in the fellowship. He had heard Shinran's teaching with his own keen ears and listening heart. Since he could not passively sit by and see the treasure of Shinran's insight lost in the morass of conflicting interpretations, he felt compelled to speak out. As the *Tannisho* itself is witness, Shinshu was enabled to be a vital and enduring tradition because concerned people looked into the issues and tried to understand what Shinran had taught.

Yuien-bo sounds an important note when he observes that the people who follow us will be the losers if the faith is not clarified and maintained. The believer has a responsibility to the future, to hand on the heritage in its purity. An aspect of religious faith is the responsibility to make it available to those who follow. We cannot merely be content that we have it and enjoy it. What are we handing on to others? Have we so understood it and practiced it that it is worthy of being transmitted? An image I like of tradition is that it is like a water pipe. We could not get the precious water we need to live if the pipes did not carry it over long distances from the reservoir. However, if the pipes become rusty and dirty, the water will be polluted. Each of us is a portion of the pipe of tradition. What is the condition of the water passing through us?

At the same time that we are responsible for the future, Yuien-bo indicates that we must be guided by a teacher. This statement is important in our present time of revolt against authority and teaching. If we look over our lives from our earliest childhood, it becomes clear that much of what we know, we have learned through the kindly guidance of some person who willingly took the time to instruct us. We are all teachers in some respect as we share thoughts and insights with others. The teacher also has a great responsibility. In this case, Yuien-bo stresses that we could not learn of the way to enlightenment unless there had been a guide who gave the essential truth.

Then Yuien-bo warns that we must not sacrifice the truth of the teaching of Other Power merely to press our self-centered views. We must look at this passage very closely in the light of our contemporary religious situation. In our day there is little in the way of intelligent religious discussion because everything is considered to be merely an expression of subjective opinion. We no longer understand that while there must be freedom for the expression of opinion and varying perceptions, the truth, however elusive, must be our goal. Opinion is not itself truth. Yuien-bo is saying that the way of faith cannot simply be what anyone wishes it to be. One cannot call something the truth which arises merely from one's subjective bias and predisposition. There has to be an interacting and interdependent relationship between one's experience and insight and the nature of the tradition. The teacher is the mediator between the tradition and pure personal experience. The guide to whom Yuien-bo appealed was Shinran, whose words had illuminated the dark religious world of that time.

While Yuien-bo places great stress on the importance of the teacher in bringing us the truth, he is not championing a dogmatic and authoritarian view of religion. Everywhere today authority is being challenged, and rightly so. It is necessary to consider what makes an authority an authority, and what role authority plays in our lives. Unfortunately, much authority in the past has been enforced in the community by means of threats of punishment.

A close reading of the *Tannisho* shows that Shinran and Yuien-bo were sensitive to the issue of authority and its effect on personal relations. Though they spoke with authority, they were not authoritarian. There are no threats, no condemnations or penalties for failure to agree. In chapter six, Shinran rejects the term deshi (disciple) as the way to describe his relationship to his followers. The terms ondobo (fellow followers) and *ondogyo* (fellow practicers of the faith) came to be used in Shinshu tradition. Authority was expressed within the context of complete equality. It was not a means to express subordination and inferiority among members. According to Shinran, each person's faith comes from the same source. Therefore, despite the fact that the teacher may have insight, he is not essentially any better than anyone else. Rather, he is more responsible to others. In his own life Shinran fulfilled the principle *Jishin kyoninshin*. This phrase means that the faith one receives, one shares with others. As we proceed through the *Tannisho*, it will become increasingly apparent that Shinran and Yuien-bo held a concept of authority that was different from that of other schools of Buddhism in that age.

The basis of Shinran's appeal to authority rests on the awareness of gratitude to the Buddha and to one's teacher. It is the authority of gratitude. In charting one's attitudes and actions, one must be aware of the debt of gratitude one owes to those who have lightened his path, who have brought the message of emancipation and freedom. Thus Shinran notes that though he does not have formal control over his disciples—that in effect he has no disciples, they in turn must consider their responsibilities to the teaching as they become aware of Amida's Vow of compassion and its meaning for their lives. Their awareness of the Vow should inspire gratitude in them and awaken their responsibility to the teaching.

This is the way of freedom and responsibility which Shinran attempted to instill in his followers. While the early community faced a multitude of issues and problems which were not easy to solve, there was a guide, a standard, for approaching those problems. It is this which Yuien-bo presents in the *Tannisho*. Yet, it is remarkable that the text is singularly lacking in demands for conformity and dogmatism.

One may ask, however, why such differences arose in the first place. Shinran's teaching was plain. We can observe from the history of religion that this has been the fate of every creative and inspiring spiritual vision. The thought and experience of creative religious sages is like a multifaceted diamond. Depending on the angle, the sparkle comes from a different facet. Shinran was a subtle religious thinker, and his thought contains many paradoxes which he admitted himself. An example is his declaration in the *Tannisho*, chapter three, that it is easier for an evil man to be saved than a good man. He notes that this is quite contrary to the usual way of thought which gives the good person an advantage over the evil person in gaining salvation. However, this usual way of thought was contrary to the intention of Amida's Vow. For Shinran, religion was not a moralistic or competitive activity by which one may show his superiority over others. Shinran's affirmation of the evil person and assurance of his salvation led some thoughtless and ego-centered persons to believe they could do evil with impunity. Though they wished to benefit from the emancipation and freedom offered in Amida's Vow, they neglected their responsibility to others by following their own egoistic impulses. It is such issues as these that are in the background of Yuien-bo's concern and which lead him to place great stress on the standard set by the teacher, Shinran, and on the responsibility believers have to the faith and to those who will receive it in later generations.

CHAPTER 3

The Essence of Shin Faith

Chapter one of the *Tannisho* is the foundation chapter, providing in concentrated form the basic principle of the Pure Land way to enlightenment and salvation. In addition, it conveys the spirit and general perspective by which Shinran approached the people of his time and his own followers. Chapter one contains all the essential terms and concepts required to explain or deal with all the issues that will follow in the text.

It begins with the source and basis of salvation, Amida Buddha and his profound Vow. The goal is rebirth (*ojo*), assured by the Vow; and the realization of this goal is through faith. The manifestation of salvation is the mind to say the Nembutsu, "*Namu-Amida-Butsu.*" Immediately upon the experience of faith and the Nembutsu, the goal is attained in the embrace of Amida Buddha, which never excludes or abandons. In actual life, the object of the Vow is the passion-ridden person whose evils are profound and whose lusts are aflame. The one essential is faith in the Vow, in comparison to which there is no superior spiritual reality, nor anything more powerful or effective in bringing beings to enlightenment.

The profound Vow of Amida Buddha refers to the story in the *Larger Pure Land Sutra* where the Bodhisattva Dharmakara, moved by the sufferings of the people in the world, determined to devote himself to finding a way of salvation for all beings. He meditated, studied, and disciplined himself in all forms of virtue through many aeons of time. Finally he achieved enlightenment and the fulfillment of his aspirations and became Amida Buddha, the Buddha of Infinite Light and Life. His land is the Western Paradise where he welcomes all beings. As the basis of his discipline and pursuit of enlightenment, Dharmakara made Forty-eight Vows which comprehend all forms of spiritual condition and destiny. They are the ideal of spiritual life. Within these Forty-eight Vows, the Eighteenth Vow became the most important for the Pure Land denominations, since it promised rebirth into Amida's Pure Land for those people who believed in and thought perhaps as many as ten thoughts concerning Amida. The thought on Amida came to be identified in tradition as the recitation of Amida's Name, infused with sacred power to purify. Hence, for many the *Namu-Amida-Butsu* was regarded as a means to salvation.

An important consideration of the Vows of Amida is what guidance they offer to religious understanding and our way of life. In modern times, some people have found it difficult to accept this story which purports to tell of events in primordial, primeval times in the cosmos. In actuality, Amida or Dharmakara was not a historical personage as we understand history. He is a mythical hero. His story represents the deepest aspirations of the human heart for the ideal condition in which all of us will experience freedom and emancipation from the conflicts and egoism that plague our lives. Amida is a symbol of reality and points to our interdependence and the need to share with others. When Dharmakara made his Vows, he put them in the form: If, when I become Buddha, all beings do not experience the same realization, then I will not accept the highest enlightenment. Dharmakara, then Amida, indicates that salvation is not a private matter, a selfish pursuit merely to save oneself. Religion as the way to enlightenment must include others and work on their behalf, or else there can be no meaning to that salvation. This principle is made the first principle of the Four Vows of the Bodhisattva which many people recite in temples today: "I vow to save all the infinite sentient beings (*Shujo muhen seigando*)." To attain this end, the Bodhisattva aspires to remove his passions, study the way and attain enlightenment. According to the *Larger Pure Land Sutra*, this all became reality with the fulfillment of each Vow by Dharmakara. Hence, in reality, salvation is not a future goal; it has already taken place.

Because salvation is already a reality, and it has come about through the fulfillment of his Vows, Shinran states in Japanese that we are "caused to be saved" by the mystery of Amida's profound Vow. The mood of the verb as causative, passive is important to observe since it is a basic principle of Shinran to see that all efforts to gain salvation root in Amida, not in our limited and defiled wills.

The goal offered by Amida's Vows is rebirth into the Pure Land. This concept is central to the Pure Land tradition, but it has been understood in various ways due to the varying levels of spiritual and intellectual insight in the people whom it addressed throughout Asia. Some undoubtedly took it literally and lived with anxiety as to whether they might reach it. Many forms of ritual developed to allay anxiety and give the people a sense that they could assist themselves or their loved ones to a better life hereafter.

More mystical or scholarly Buddhist teachers, in harmony with the non-duality of Buddha and the world, realized that there was no separate world of Amida, but that Amida may be the heart of the reality in which we live. For them the truth of the Pure Land and Amida Buddha is seen in the eternal aspiration of all humanity for a higher, more lasting spiritual existence. This aspiration is sometimes turned to pursuit of egoistic goals as the way to satisfy the deeper spiritual longings of the soul. Rebirth as the mythological-symbolic way of expressing enlightenment takes place in the moment that one glimpses the true source of spiritual emancipation and realization. When one transcends his egoism, even for a short moment in his life, he senses the possibility of a new life. Our human problem is how to transform these occasional moments of spiritual exaltation and insight into a more permanent and enduring condition.

In short, although Pure Land teaching developed on the popular level as a religion of salvation in the future life, in its deepest understanding Pure Land teaching points to the conditions which undergird even our present life as the way to enlightenment. It embodies a philosophy for living creatively in this world.

The next major term in this passage is faith. This concept is the heart of Shinran's teaching and the unique feature of Shinshu among all Buddhist schools. According to Shinran's interpretation of the Eighteenth Vow, Amida had promised the fulfillment of all essentials of salvation. The three elements in traditional Pure Land teaching for gaining rebirth were sincerity, faith, and aspiration for birth in the Pure Land. Shinran declared that these elements were transferred, conferred, or given to the person by Amida Buddha. Thus he made faith the center of salvation and understood it as the true mind, the true and real mind of Amida, becoming manifest within us. With this concept Shinran gave a new direction and meaning to religion and religious experience in Japanese tradition. His insight ranks him among the most perceptive sages of religious history.

At the moment we believe, Shinran notes also that a mind, or impulse, to say the Nembutsu arises within the person. We must carefully study this passage since interpretations vary concerning its meaning. Many people place emphasis on the recitation of the Nembutsu referred to in the sentence. However, the structure of the sentence shows that it is the mind, the state of mind, which is of central interest. Shinran affirmed the practice of the Nembutsu, but its meaning was determined by the state of mind in the believer and what he believed he was doing when he recited the Nembutsu.

In tradition, the recitation of the Nembutsu was used as a way of gaining merit or purifying one from karmic sins. It is said in the *Meditation Sutra* of the Pure Land School that a recitation of the Name would purify one from eight billions of aeons of sins. Like other mantras, sometimes the Nembutsu was used in a magical way to gain benefits. With Honen Shonin, the practice of reciting the Nembutsu became the sole means to gain salvation in the decadent ages of *Mappo* (Final Dharma) when Buddhism was to decline and disappear completely. This was an ancient theory which was widely believed in Japan at that time. According to Honen, the mere recitation of the Nembutsu would bring salvation. The essential elements of sincerity, faith, and desire for birth would naturally arise by themselves. In a way, Honen taught that doing is believing. There were many critics of Honen; and Shinran, his disciple, tried to clarify Honen's teaching by distinguishing between self-power Nembutsu and Other Power Nembutsu.

According to Shinran, self-power Nembutsu is used by a person to gain his own salvation. Other Power Nembutsu is really a summons by Amida to humans, aroused in them as a sign that they are already saved. Underlying this distinction was Shinran's realization that in order for the recitation of the Name to have meaning, it must be rooted in deep faith—and it was that faith which saved. Thus he could meet the criticisms of the Zen master Dogen (1200–53), who claimed that Pure Land people merely mouthed words and mumbled incantations, with the reply that in the Nembutsu was proclaimed the truth of *zazen*.

Shinran spiritualized the practice of Nembutsu as the sign of salvation. He removed it from the sphere of obligation, and regarded it as a spontaneous expression of gratitude. It was no longer a means to an end, a tool, but a sign of the end itself. In the *Kyogyoshinsho*, a monumental work of Shinran, he notes that the Nembutsu does not produce faith, but it is faith that produces or expresses itself in the Nembutsu. It is faith, and not the Nembutsu, as simply recitation, which is the basis of salvation.

When the mind which believes and is moved to recite the Nembutsu appears, in that very moment we are embraced, never to be rejected or excluded. This is the moment when destiny is sealed, according to Shinran. There is no need to wait until some distant future to gain emancipation. In the sentence describing this in the *Tannisho* there is used a little word, *sunawachi, soku*, which has an extremely important meaning. In Buddhism the term *soku* means "identity," "simultaneously," "no interval of time in between." In other texts, Shinran frequently comments on this term and stresses that when faith is experienced, that is identical to, and simultaneous with, rebirth in the Pure Land. This assurance that comes with faith is important in religious life because it removes all anxiety concerning our future. We all have this anxiety because of our constant imperfection and unstable commitments. It has been observed by scholars that in later times, Shinshu followers such as the Omi merchants could devote their time to dealing with affairs in this world because their futures were secure in the world hereafter.

It is interesting to note here that theologians and philosophers are frequently criticized for splitting hairs and making subtle distinctions. Perhaps sometimes they are just playing games. However, in the case of Shinran, the interpretation and use of terms, though "hairsplitting" and subtle, opened the way to new and vital interpretations of Buddhism in his time, and for ours, interpretations of tremendous practical importance for daily living and human relations both then and now.

CHAPTER **4**

Faith and Reality

As we have already noted, the arising of faith and the impulse to recite the Nembutsu are simultaneous expressions of the embrace which never excludes. This embrace and non-exclusion refer to the all embracing compassion of Amida Buddha and are symbolized by light. Amida is the Buddha of Infinite Light. The light of Buddha is a fitting symbol for a religion of absolute compassion, for just as the light of the sun illuminates the world without excluding anything, so universal and non-discriminating is Buddha's light.

The symbol of light is a fundamental figure in all universal religions. The sun, as the source of light for our world, is also the basis of our life in the world. Thus light and life are associated together. According to the sutras, Amida is the Buddha of Infinite Light and Life. It is also a fitting symbol for Other Power, because no matter how sharp our sight might be, without the light it would be impossible to see. The *Meditation Sutra* gives us a description of the breadth of Amida's Light:

> Buddha Amitayus has eighty-four thousand signs of perfection, each sign is possessed of eighty-four minor marks of excellence, each mark has eighty-four thousand rays, each ray extends so far as to shine over the world of the ten quarters, whereby Buddha embraces and protects all beings who think upon him and does not exclude any of them.[1]

In Buddhist tradition, light stands for wisdom. It is frequently presented in sutras as a stream of light coming from the Buddha and illuminating every aspect of the cosmos. In modern terms, it means to see things as they really are. Because Buddha sees things as they really are, he is able to assist all beings to enlightenment, despite their delusions and ignorance. The Twelfth Vow of Amida Buddha promises that there will be no place in the universe where his light will not penetrate. Hence his universality is implied in his Name, Amida, Buddha of Infinite Light.

In religious experience, we know we have been embraced by the light of Amida as our passion-ridden condition becomes known to us and as we are stirred by the faith and hope that Amida embraces us just as we are, with all our sins and with a limitless unconscious potential for evil lurking in our subconscious depths. It may seem a platitude to state that Amida causes us to know that we are sinners and evil. Everyone is aware that he or she has some limitation and is imperfect. However, if one looks closely at general human behavior, we spend a lot of time justifying our behavior and defending our rightness against all comers. The nakedly honest fact of human existence is pride and egoism. While we may casually, for reasons of tact, admit to some small flaw, we all consider ourselves paragons of virtue compared to the person next to us. Most people do not need others to praise their own virtue; they can handle it themselves and usually do.

The illumination of our true natures, which Shinran relates, means a real existential and profound insight into our egoism and the humble recognition that we have nothing to commend ourselves when we see ourselves in the Light of Amida Buddha. This is the true basis of egolessness in Shinran's thought and experience.

The embrace of light reveals our true natures. Non-exclusion tells us that we are accepted as we are, and in spite of those evils which we cannot escape. Here another feature of Shinran's view of religion comes to the fore. Repeatedly, he lets us know that Amida's compassion is not dictated by our being good or evil. His compassion is not something we work for or merit. It is given to us without qualification. In later passages of the *Tannisho* we shall see the importance of this insight for Shinran—and for ourselves.

There is a feature of non-exclusion which reveals how absolute Shinran believed Amida's compassion to be. In the sutra relating the Eighteenth Vow, there is a clause tacked on to the end of it to the effect that people who commit the five grave sins or slander the Dharma will be excluded from the Vow. By placing such limits, this moralistic phrase appears to be in contradiction to the compassion of Amida. Yet, it became part of the sacred text and it became a problem for later Pure Land teachers who discovered that Amida's compassion was limitless. Almost as though Shinran could hear someone say that there would be exclusion of certain evildoers, he follows the declaration of the embrace and non-exclusion with the unequivocal statement that Amida's Vow does not select persons on the basis of youth or age or of goodness or evil. Faith alone is the essential qualification. In the *Kyogyoshinsho* he gives an even more explicit statement of the non-discriminating character of the Vow and faith:

> As I contemplate the ocean-like Great Faith, I see that it does not choose between the noble and the mean, the priest and the layman, nor does it discriminate between man and woman. The amount of sin is not questioned and the length of practice is not discussed. It is neither 'practice' nor 'good', neither 'abrupt' nor 'gradual', neither 'right meditation' nor 'wrong meditation', neither 'contemplative' nor 'non-contemplative', neither 'while living' nor 'at the end of life', neither 'many utterances' nor 'one thought'. Faith is the inconceivable, indescribable, and ineffable Serene Faith. It is like the *agada* which destroys all poisons. The medicine of the Tathagata's Vow destroys the *poisons of wisdom and ignorance.*[2]

Thus Shinran emphasizes that the Vow does not choose between social classes, between priests and laymen, between sexes, or by age. There are no distinctions as to discipline, no distinction as to form, no heresy or orthodoxy.

When applied to the nature of religion as it is usually practiced in every tradition, the meaning of this passage is far-reaching. In it, Shinran is saying that as a standard of membership or rank in the system, the terms and criteria commonly used to measure an individual's religious activity have no relevance when it comes to the real meaning of faith and enlightenment offered by Amida Buddha. Since Amida is the source of all faith, the external criteria and forms applied by people confuse the issue, and make religion simply a cloak for one's ego. Despite profound teachings of compassion and wisdom, all these distinctions are competitive and can lead to strife and hatred. Shinran had direct knowledge of the results of traditional religiosity from his experience on Mt. Hiei. Later, the persecution he suffered along with his master was brought about not by the politics of the government but by the religious authorities of his day, upon whom the government relied.

In our day most people believe that one religion is as good as the other, and so they are either very tolerant or rather indifferent and apathetic. In his day, Shinran understood that some ways activate ego and create conflict. He taught that it is the ideal of Amida to move people beyond these petty interests. Shinran believed that truth was an important issue to consider in religion. The mark of truth was the extent to which one gave oneself, like Amida, to the embrace which does not discriminate or exclude.

There is considerable discussion of the important concept of Voidness and non-duality in traditional Buddhism. However, for Shinran, true non-duality goes beyond all the petty distinctions we use to classify and judge people. Only when we have given up this practice of classifying and judging others and ourselves, can true unity, oneness of spirit, arise among us, and faith as a liberating reality vitalize our daily lives.

The reason for the fact that the Vow does not discriminate between good or evil people in terms of salvation is that all beings are profoundly evil and are consumed with passion.

This assertion by Shinran may appear to be extremely pessimistic and negative concerning human nature. Yet, it is a point of view which roots deeply in Buddhist teaching as well as a fact rooted in Shinran's own everyday experience.

According to Buddhism, all people are deluded through their fundamental ignorance, greed, lust, and anger. These characteristics combine to form the egoism which we all have. Any observer of life will see this is not pessimistic but realistic. How else can we explain the problems of the world? Shinran observed these qualities in himself even during the time when he practiced Buddhism on Mt. Hiei. Recognition of his defiled nature and its resistance to change through religious discipline led him to Honen and eventually to his own insights on the way to salvation. Believing that we can be emancipated, Shinran was an optimist. He wrote of himself as he looked back over his experience:

> Truly I know. Sad is it that I, Gutoku Ran, sunk in the vast sea of lust and lost in the great mountain of desire for fame and profit, do not rejoice in joining the group of the Rightly Established State, nor do I enjoy coming near the True Enlightenment. What a shame! What a sorrow![3]

Such was his realism, but he also expresses optimism rooted in Amida's Vow:

> What a joy it is that I place my mind in the soil of the Buddha's Universal Vow and I let my thoughts flow into the sea of the Inconceivable Dharma. I deeply acknowledge the Tathagata's Compassion and sincerely appreciate the master's (Honen's) benevolence in instructing me.[4]

This chapter of the *Tannisho* (chapter one) ends on a note of victory and optimism which has many implications. Shinran boldly declares that nothing more than faith is required. For him, religion is totally an inner condition. It is a matter of spirit. No other good is required. There is no good that excels the Nembutsu. We are to fear no evil because no evil can obstruct or hinder the effectiveness of the Vow.

What evils does he refer to? Opinions vary, but perhaps personal evils—no matter how bad or seemingly incorrigible we are, this does not prevent the Vow from saving us. Or, in the light of the persecution of Pure Land teaching, it might mean that nothing in the world can keep the Vow from bringing salvation to everyone. We need have no fears of our own imperfections, or of the effect of troubles in the world, for Amida's Vow of compassion is the only true reality and basis for the meaning of life. Such, as given in this short chapter, was Shinran's faith. Though short, this chapter, as is characteristic of each chapter in the *Tannisho*, reaches far into reality.

CHAPTER **5**

Experience and Communication

Chapter one in the *Tannisho* announces the fundamental principles of faith in Amida's Vow. It is a declaration of faith. Chapter two deals with the problem of faith as it is experienced and communicated.

The occasion behind chapter two appears to be a visit to Shinran by some of his disciples who, despite many dangers which lay along that road, travelled from eastern Japan over ten provinces to reach Kyoto. They wished to know from Shinran whether there was more to his teaching than he had taught them earlier when, years before, he lived in the Kanto area. The chapter is thus a defense of Shinran's understanding of faith in Amida and an explanation of how this faith is related to the Buddhist tradition. Chapter two is, in essence, a very personal statement to show where Shinran stands.

Why was it necessary for his disciples to make this trip and question the teacher on his understanding? Why did Shinran declare himself in no uncertain terms to express this position? Here we must look into the history of the early Shinshu community.

Shinran studied with Honen from 1201 to about 1207. During this period he underwent a religious transformation which he never forgot, and his relation to Honen was ever after the hinge-point of his life. This is reflected in the *Tannisho* chapter two as well as the *Kyogyoshinsho*. From about 1207 to 1211 Shinran, like Honen, was exiled. He went to Echigo, a northern province that is now the area of Niigata, while Honen went to Tosa in Shikoku. They never met again. Pardoned in 1211, Shinran stayed in Echigo, but in 1213 he left for the Kanto area where he entered into evangelistic activity. As a result of this, he gathered numerous followers. Then, after a period of roughly twenty years, for unknown reasons, Shinran returned to Kyoto in about 1235 and remained there until his death in 1262.

As we pointed out earlier, Shinran's teaching contains paradoxes and subtleties which, without careful reflection and probing of one's own experience, could be misunderstood. His letters show that conflicts arose over the meaning of the way of salvation and its ethical implications. In order to deal with this problem, he dispatched his eldest son, Zenran, as his representative. After some time it became apparent that Zenran was claiming Shinran had given him a special teaching which he had not given to others. On the authority of representing his father, he wanted to control the Kanto followers and even accused some to his father. Eventually the truth became clear and Shinran had to excommunicate and disown his son. It was a great blow to him, this tragedy which took place about 1256.

The exact nature of Zenran's teaching is unclear. He claimed that what had been previously taught by Shinran was a faded flower. From this single clue scholars suggest that he may have been legalistic, encouraging practices of purification and cultivation of virtue in addition to the Nembutsu. In later times, Zenran was depicted as a leader of fortune tellers and sorcerers, so it is possible that he also combined Pure Land teaching with popular superstitions from the many folk religions of Japan.

Although the events of this time are not entirely clear, the hints that we have give background to the problem confronting Shinran on the occasion of the disciples' visit as described by Yuien-bo in the *Tannisho*'s chapter two. It was an urgent visit, which they undertook despite many difficulties in travel. What they wanted to know was: what else besides the Nembutsu is required for salvation?

Shinran's immediate response, from which he never deviated, was that there is nothing else than the Nembutsu as the way of rebirth into the Pure Land. He tells them that to think he knows or teaches anything else is a great mistake. He goes on to declare that if faith is reduced to a content of knowledge, then it would be better to seek out scholars in Nara and Mt. Hiei, where the most noted and greatest Buddhist scholars are located. Then one may hear from them the essential teachings about the way of rebirth in the Pure Land.

This statement is important because it emphasizes that faith or salvation is not merely a matter of information or even belief in the form of intellectual assent. Gathering information, passages, and teachings may appear to give strength to a belief or proof, but that is not itself the root of faith. Faith is something different, something deeper.

The second point to notice is that Shinran recognizes that other schools teach Pure Land doctrine and can outline the essentials for birth in the Pure Land. In fact, Pure Land teaching was propagated by all major schools of Buddhism in China and Japan as a secondary way of salvation for the common people, who could not engage in the more rigorous and demanding monastic life and methods of meditation. The varieties of Pure Land teaching made it necessary for Shinran to clarify his own position on its meaning.

Thirdly, in a very strong way, Shinran highlights his own position. "As for me, Shinran (*Shinran ni okite wa*)"—he singles himself out. By using his own name, he declares firmly that there is no other way than to believe what he has received from Honen: that we are saved by Amida through the Nembutsu. Thus he places himself clearly with Honen and sole reliance on Nembutsu.

Several times in the *Tannisho* Shinran refers personally to himself in order to place in high contrast his position and that of others. Here he emphasizes his adherence to Honen's teaching. In chapter five, he declares that I, Shinran (unlike others), have never said the Nembutsu once out of filial piety. In chapter six, I, Shinran (unlike others), have not even one disciple. We may note a decisiveness and forthrightness in Shinran in taking his stand. He had self-confidence, though he was not dogmatic or judgmental and pompous.

By this means, Shinran points to an important element of religious life. Our religious life is something on which we stake our lives. It is not mere belief or information, but is identified with our existence itself. Thus when Shinran says "I, Shinran ..." it is not that he is stating a theory but it is the texture and essence of his own life that is being expressed. He is saying in essence: I am my religion, I am my faith; my religion is myself and my faith is myself. There is no split between faith and life.

Because they compartmentalize their lives, modern people have difficulty in confronting such figures as Shinran. Religion is something one may do on a special day or special time. It must compete with other activities of life for attention. However, in the truly religious person, as illustrated by Shinran, religion is what one is at every moment of his life and in every relationship. It is the spirit and quality of that life. It is what determines the focus of that life.

We modern men and women suffer from fragmentation in our lives. We experience frustration with the numberless demands made upon our lives and emotions by the fast pace of contemporary events. As the world has shrunk because of modern means of communication and travel, the strain has become greater on each one of us, whose mind and emotions are constantly assaulted by the sufferings and problems of people everywhere. As a participant in society, a member of a family, owner, partner, or employee in a business, recipient or initiator of a friendship, there are countless demands made on our time and energies. What will put all this into focus? How can we achieve integration in our lives and experience ourselves as whole persons? For Shinran, such focus, such integration, resulted from the way of faith which he first learned from Honen.

CHAPTER 6

Theory Versus Life

Shinran's answer to the questions of those who had traveled at the risk of their lives across ten provinces was the deeply personal and unequivocal declaration that the single essential was faith in the Nembutsu as taught by the "good man," Honen. In his own view, Shinran was merely a transmitter of that truth. He reaffirms in no uncertain terms the sole practice of the Nembutsu as the principle for which he, like Honen, had given his life energies to spread among the people. Pointing to his own experience, Shinran indicates that he had found the focus of his life in the Nembutsu as the expression of faith in Amida's salvation. To him, any other view was simply in error. He declared:

> As for me, Shinran, I can only accept what my venerable master Honen said: "Just say the Nembutsu and be saved by Amida."

While Honen may have been a mild person, his teaching on the Nembutsu had become very controversial. His radical departure from Buddhist tradition was that he did not teach the Nembutsu as simply one practice among the many practices which had developed from Gautama's teachings. Rather, he maintained that the Nembutsu, the recitation of Amida Buddha's Name, was the one single practice suitable to people of this decadent and corrupt age.

According to Honen, Amida Buddha's Vow, in establishing the practice of the Nembutsu, promised salvation for all people, high or low, good or evil. Of all Buddhist practices—from meditation and precepts to building temples, making images, or copying sutras—only the Nembutsu was truly universal and open to everyone regardless of ability or character. It was characteristic of Honen's interpretation of Amida's compassion that it was inclusive rather than exclusive. The final chapters of the *Tannisho*, in which Yuien-bo rejects any discriminating criterion that contradicts the universality of Amida's Vow, gives practical expression to Honen's ideal.

The traditional schools of Nara and Mt. Hiei severely criticized Honen's teachings outlined in his major text, *The Treatise on the Nembutsu of the Select Original Vow*. They accused Honen of distorting Pure Land teaching and Buddhism and, together with his major disciples—Shinran among them—exiled Honen from Kyoto. Later, hostility towards Honen was so great that his enemies desecrated his grave. For a long time, Pure Land teaching was persecuted as a subversive teaching.

Knowing of these attacks and this background of antagonism from the Buddhist centers at Nara, Mt. Hiei, and the tradition-oriented powers in the secular government, we can better understand Shinran's declarations that he does not know ultimately whether the Nembutsu is the seed that will lead to birth in the Pure Land or the karmic action that will result in his falling into hell. We should note here the careful choice of words—the Nembutsu as a "seed"—a positive potential that grows and eventually bears fruit, and at the same time the negative karmic deed that drags one down to hell. In this same passage, Shinran goes on to state that while Honen might have been wrong, and he, Shinran, might have been misled, this could only be an occasion for regret if Shinran were truly able to gain enlightenment through his own fulfillment of the demands of traditional Buddhist discipline and practice. But from his own experience Shinran had learned he could not perform those practices or achieve the necessary perfection and purity to attain enlightenment by that "path of the sages." Thus, in any case, without Honen's Nembutsu teaching and its hope, Shinran would be destined for hell. If Honen was ultimately proved wrong, Shinran would not have lost anything by following his teaching, since he could do nothing else anyway!

The issue here is theory versus life. If one tried to prove the Nembutsu from an intellectual standpoint alone, there would be no way to prove that in contrast to some other approach, it brings enlightenment. Shinran's advice to his questioners in chapter two is that if one wishes to engage in a theoretical and intellectual analysis of the problem of salvation, they should visit the scholars in Nara or on Mt. Hiei.

For Shinran, the rightness or wrongness of Honen's teachings was more than an intellectual issue or a game. It was a question of his existence—of his very life. Concentrated in his terse statement in chapter two was his reflection on twenty years of experience in which he had attempted to fulfill the ideals of Buddhist discipline and completely failed. His intense spiritual anxiety and frustration had led him to a period of seclusion and meditation in the Rokkakudo in Kyoto and finally to Honen's hermitage, where he found spiritual release, and assurance of his salvation, through faith in the Nembutsu. Though Shinran may have first studied this teaching on Mt. Hiei, it was in Honen's hermitage that it became real to him.

Throughout his long lifetime as a practicer of the Nembutsu, Shinran spoke from his own personal experience to those he taught. In facing up to the meaning of his spiritual imperfection, he looks deeply into his own heart. Scattered among his writings are numerous confessions where he describes his persistent and ineradicably passionate nature. What he describes is the heart of all humanity, for all people—when they can be honest with themselves—realize their moments of lust and passion and thus in the timelessness of human feelings, Shinran strikes a universal chord of sympathy. We see clearly in the *Tannisho*, and in Shinran's own writings, that he was a realistic and honest person who tried to see himself for what he really was. The deeper he probed the nature of his own human imperfection, the more real and embracing became his awareness of Amida's compassion and Vow. Faith in Amida's Vow was the key to final salvation. Thus in the light of his experience and his insight into Amida's Vow, Shinran would give little weight to any intellectual attempt to prove or disprove Honen's teaching.

The form of argument which Shinran employs in explaining why he follows that teaching is an argument arising from practical religious consciousness. The Nembutsu is the last resort open to passion-ridden people like Shinran. It is an argument similar to Pascal's wager concerning the existence of God in Christianity. According to Pascal, one cannot lose anything by believing in God, though one might lose everything if he disbelieves and it turns out that God really exists. Of course, no one really believes in God or the Nembutsu on this coldly calculating, businesslike basis. Both arguments show that whatever intellectual merits there may be in the issue, a person is still faced with the fundamental decision on the question of his destiny. Each one seeks desperately for some basis of hope and assurance. If only intellectual arguments were available to demonstrate faith, the spiritual life would be greatly impoverished and, being based on fear, would be very negative as well.

Shinran having exposed the uselessness of such arguments, proceeds to the positive dimension of faith—the true foundation of his joy and hope. He states that if the Vow of Amida is true, then Shakyamuni's teaching is true, and in turn Zendo's and Honen's and finally his own principles which he draws from that spiritual lineage. For Shinran, the stream of truth represented in Pure Land tradition hangs on the reality of Amida's Vow. When this Vow is experienced, the truth of the teaching becomes clear. The limited question which he takes up earlier in chapter two about whether Honen had misled him is now shifted to a vaster perspective—the reality of the Vow of Amida. If that Vow exists truly, then what has been taught through history is not false or empty, for these teachers have attempted to make clear the embracing compassion of Amida's Vow. The inner experience of profound compassion is the witness to the reality of the Vow. Teachings which make real that compassion all derive from the Vow itself.

Shinran placed his faith in the Vow of Amida as a result of his own personal experience, something that cannot be proven or disproven by intellectual analysis. Faith has to be experienced. Nothing external can coerce it. It is interesting and significant to note that Shinran ends the discussion in a sensitive way, consistent with his understanding that faith derives from the Vow. In a gentle fashion he declares: "And now, whether you entrust yourself to the Nembutsu or reject it is entirely up to you."

CHAPTER **7**

The Transformation of Faith

The *Tannisho*, chapter three, contains perhaps not only the most famous and striking parts of the entire text, but also the most famous passage among Shinran's writings. It has gained wide notoriety because in it, in the clearest fashion, Shinran revealed the paradoxical and radical character of his thought and interpretations of Buddhist and Pure Land teaching. He declares:

> Even a good person can be born in the Pure Land, how much more so an evil person!

Then he admits that this is really quite contrary to the way people usually think.

> However, people commonly say, "Even an evil person can be born in the Pure Land, how much more so a good person!"

According to Shinran, the world's view of salvation contradicts the meaning and purpose of the Original Vow and does not truly represent Pure Land teaching. Here Shinran poses the question of the meaning of religion in its clearest terms. What is the purpose of salvation? Is it to congratulate the righteous, or to give hope to the hopeless? In this chapter, Shinran specifically makes a point of asserting that "Since his [i.e., Amida's] purpose was to enable people like us to attain Buddhahood, it is particularly the evil person who completely entrusts himself to Other Power who will be born in the Pure Land."

In order to appreciate Shinran's interpretation, we must place his statements in the context of the development of Buddhism. We can see that Shinran's teaching was the logical outcome of the Buddhist definition of the human condition. At the same time, Shinran carried that logic forward on the basis of his own existential experience of attempting to attain perfection through Buddhist disciplines for a period of twenty years on Mt. Hiei.

Buddhism has always defined the human condition as enmeshed in profound ignorance and delusion. This fundamental condition produces the egoism, greed, hatred, and lusts that are the source of all forms of suffering in the world. However, Buddhist teachers and followers throughout the centuries believed that they could gain release through their own efforts and discipline, following the example of Gautama Buddha. With the development of Mahayana Buddhism there came the recognition that the compassion of the Buddhas and Bodhisattvas reaches out to assist suffering beings in their progress toward enlightenment. At the same time the awareness of human inability to attain perfection through one's own limited efforts became intensified with the doctrine of the last age in the decline of the Dharma, during which the beneficial influence of Buddhism would weaken and fade away. The stage was set for the appearance of Pure Land teaching, which spread widely in China and then Japan as a teaching of hope in a dark and corrupt world.

However, until Shinran's time, the basic assumption of all forms of Buddhism was that good deeds bring salvation, whether they be rigorous practices of meditation or the simple practice of reciting the Nembutsu as much as possible. All forms of good deeds produced merit leading eventually to enlightenment.

Shinran's experience of personal frustration and failure in the pursuit of good deeds opened his eyes to the real issue of salvation and enlightenment. He observed that the goal of Buddhism was to enable the individual to attain the state of egolessness, to be purified of egoism or egocentrism. He saw that there was an inner contradiction in the various noble and pious efforts of religious people, because they were all done in the expectation of personal or egoistic benefits or merit. Thus Shinran recognized that good deeds were poisonous and obstructions to true enlightenment when done in the proud awareness that they were good. He concluded that if every pious or noble deed is itself essentially egoistic, then no pious or noble deed can free us from the ignorance, passion, and egoism that bind us to the cycles of rebirth.

Shinran has written at great length concerning this issue in the volume on *Faith* in the *Kyogyoshinsho*:

> All the ocean-like multitudinous beings, since the beginningless past, have been transmigrating in the sea of ignorance, drowning in the cycle of existence, bound to the cycle of sufferings, and having no pure, serene faith. They have as a natural consequence, no true serene faith. Therefore, it is difficult to meet the highest virtue and difficult to receive the supreme, pure Faith. All the common and petty persons at all times constantly defile their good minds with greed and lust, and their anger and hatred constantly burn the treasure of the Dharma. Even though they work and practice as busily as though they were sweeping fire off their heads, their practices are called poisoned and mixed good deeds and also called deluded and deceitful practices; hence, they are not called true acts. If one desires to be born in the Land of Infinite Light with these deluded and poisoned good, he cannot possibly attain it.[1]

Stimulated by this insight, Shinran realized that the fulfillment of Amida's Original Vow to save all suffering sentient beings was not dependent on their performance of good deeds. Rather, it is clearly the purpose of the Vow to save those who could not save themselves. Hence, Shinran maintained that the aim of Amida's Vow was to save evil persons, not good ones (if there were any).

Shinran should not be misinterpreted here as rejecting doing good deeds or advocating doing evil deeds. For him the problem lay not in the action itself, but in the mind or attitude attending the action. According to Shinran, the reason that good deeds might become an obstruction to enlightenment is that "those who believe that they themselves have the power to perform good acts are not inclined to rely completely on Other Power ..." He goes on, "However, if they abandon their attachment to self-power and entrust themselves completely to Other Power, then they, too, will be born in the True Land of Recompense." In effect, Shinran is focusing on the motive, the way of understanding our actions.

Shinran clearly understood that people must live and act in this world. However, our actions should not be considered for the merit they bring or the contribution they may make toward our future enlightenment. Religion is not a matter of calculation or self-glorification. Rather in Shinran's teaching all actions are to be considered as expressions of gratitude for the compassion that we have received even when undeserving. Reliance on Other Power means a life of thankfulness which recognizes that in all areas of our lives we are more receivers than we are givers. It is the life lived in the awareness that the small, petty good deeds that we do cannot compare with the profound compassion with which the cosmos, nature, family, and other people surround us. Such a mind, such an awareness, is the true basis of humility. Humility can only arise from a deep sense of limitedness and imperfection. People become proud of their humility when they view it as a good in themselves. Shinran, however, points the way to true egolessness which arises when we become deeply and truly aware of our imperfection and boundedness and at the same time perceive the deep compassion in reality that sustains us, despite our imperfections.

Shinran is noteworthy because he shifted the center of gravity of religion from the quantitative to the qualitative, from forms of religion to the spirit of religion. According to Shinran, the experience of faith within ourselves is the result of Amida Buddha's endowing us with his mind of truth and purity. Faith signifies a transformation of our minds so that we come to full realization of our true natures as human beings and the true source of the good that supports our lives. Thus in his letters, Shinran indicates that the number of Nembutsu one recites is no real issue. He writes: "As you are assured in your mind that your rebirth is completely determined, there is nothing else to do but to recite the Nembutsu sincerely when you contemplate the Buddha's benevolence."[2]

Although Shinran is dealing largely in metaphysical principles in an effort to make clear the meaning of faith in Amida Buddha, there are ethical implications involved in his thought. The model of compassion indicated in the story of Amida Buddha points the way to our own approach to human problems. The myth tells us that reality does not measure its relation to us by what we deserve. It follows its own principle of absolute compassion in nurturing life. Society is contradictory in proposing that people be compassionate and at the same time calculate what they deserve. It is not particularly a mark of compassion merely to give someone what they deserve. Rather, it is true compassion to see beyond the deserving into the true nature of the person. The principle of compassion forgives the deed in the hope of liberating the humanity. Revenge and vengeance is not a sign of compassion, but there is always the possibility that forgiveness and acceptance may liberate oneself and the other, however apparently undeserving.

CHAPTER 8

Action and Compassion

Chapter four introduces the distinction between the compassion of the Holy Path, the "path of sages and saints," and the Pure Land Path. The difference corresponds to the distinction between self-power and Other Power which we have already encountered in the text. It is a distinction which grows out of an understanding of the total inability of any individual to attain salvation or enlightenment by means of the various practices of traditional Buddhism, an interpretation based on Shinran's realization that all good deeds have a core of egoism because everyone expects to receive benefits from their good acts. Any form of practice based on such attitudes is insufficient and incomplete and cannot assure a person of final liberation. Shinran makes clear that by contrast, the Pure Land way—founded on faith in Amida's Vow—brings assurance of final liberation, because it illumines our human limitations and arouses deeper awareness of the reality of Amida's compassion. Pure Land faith sets forth a dialectic in which the more we sense our imperfection, the more compassion at the heart of reality—which Amida Buddha symbolizes—becomes real. Paradoxically, the more undeserving of salvation one feels, the more salvation is guaranteed. Conversely, the more one believes and strives to gain it, on one's own efforts and abilities, the further the goal recedes.

This paradox has its psychological foundation in human experience. Sometimes, the more we struggle for a solution to a problem, the more impossible the problem becomes. It is only by ceasing to strive, and by standing back from the problem, that it may be solved. Striving which arouses ego-investment may bring failure when the intent to succeed blinds a person to important facets of the issue. Striving also creates artificiality and superficiality. It is a great source of hypocrisy in religion when one tries to be pious or humble.

Shinran's experience taught him the limitations of struggle or striving for enlightenment. He recognized that only when the striving ceased could the true power that liberates become realized in our lives. Thus his many confessions express his awareness of imperfection and also the joyous experience of the embrace which does not reject offered by Amida Buddha.

On the background of Shinran's own awareness, the distinction between the two forms of compassion has importance for our approach to life and religion. Compassion means altruism, or concern for others. It involves, in some measure, a desire to do good for others. The Bodhisattva in Mahayana Buddhism is the major symbol of this compassion. It was out of compassion for all suffering beings that the Bodhisattva Dharmakara (Hozo) established the Forty-eight Vows and became Amida Buddha. All forms of Buddhism provide means whereby a person can express his compassion through the practice of eko or transfer of merit. The eko is an element of every religious service. As Shinran noticed, however, in the path of the sages, "In this present life, it is hard to save others, no matter how much love and pity we feel towards them. Thus our compassion is limited and ephemeral." In his letters Shinran appears to acknowledge that Nembutsu said on behalf of others may bring them benefit. He did not wish to reject expressions of concern for others. Nevertheless, he saw that even such Nembutsu were insufficient because of the instability of human feeling and because the scope of beings in need exceeded the ability of people to fulfill by their own finite practices. From Shinran's standpoint, it was impossible to save himself. It could hardly be expected that one could save others.

Again, however, the Pure Land teaching gave hope, the hope that the perfect compassion of the Buddha would lead all beings to enlightenment. There need now be no anxiety concerning the final destiny of others. The absolute compassion of Amida Buddha makes unnecessary the practices performed out of anxiety for the welfare of other people in the hereafter.

Shinran also stresses that the end or goal of religion is the salvation of others and not merely our own salvation. Our goal is to become a Buddha so that we can extend mercy to others infinitely. Thus he says,

> In the Pure Land path, compassion is expressed by saying the Nembutsu; quickly attaining Buddhahood through birth in the Pure Land; and then with a great compassionate and merciful heart, bestowing merits on all sentient beings to one's heart's desire.

Hence, recitation of the Nembutsu is an expression of the mind of compassion which yearns for the final liberation of all beings. Shinran carefully directs our attention away from the pursuit of our own salvation to the ultimate basis of salvation of all beings. Along with the Nembutsu of gratitude, the Nembutsu of great compassion, as taught by Shinran, stands as a mark and milestone of the spiritualization of Buddhism and of all religion. Shinran purged faith of any implication of egoistic, self-centered concerns and practices.

In the broader ethical sphere, there is an important consideration of human activity implied in Shinran's distinction between the two forms of compassion. He recognized that everyone has an aspiration, in some way, to help others at some time in their lives. When we try to help others, we may become frustrated and end in despair because our acts fall short of solving problems or really helping people. The problem in doing good is not in knowing to do good, but in *knowing how* to do good and how to understand doing good. Shinran shows us that when we act, as we must constantly do in the world, we must understand the limited and inadequate nature of our acts in the light of Amida's absolute perfection and compassion. We should not, however, give up doing good where we can, but we should recognize that the final outcome and meaning of what we do lies in the nature of things. Compassionate action joins with the compassionate heart of reality which we find in the depth of our own being. In effect, we must live and act in the world with hopes but no expectations. We must have commitments but not demands. We should act but not strive.

This understanding of action and compassion is important because of the traditional and prevalent impression that Pure Land teaching and tradition lack social awareness. However, a survey of Pure Land teaching and its symbolism reveals that it embodies a deep concern for the well-being of all beings. Ancient and modern Buddhists have frequently engaged in a wide variety of activities to give substance to the Buddha's compassion within the world.

In our modern situation, we must recognize that an essential aspect of the application of compassion is justice. Compassion means that we seek to enhance the life of persons and to enable them to experience life richly and meaningfully. There can be no meaningful existence when people are deprived of justice and no compassion that does not attempt to implement justice.

However, the deep awareness of our own egoism and the limitations of self-generated actions cautions us not to become proud of our doing good or to consider that we have all the final solutions. It also shows us that compassion is not merely a sentiment but a way of acting. Faith provides a realism and openness which is the only means to deal with issues in a world of strife and striving.

CHAPTER **9**

Buddhist Views of Morality

In the *Tannisho*, chapter five, Shinran makes an astounding statement when he declares that *he*—he personally—has never even once said the Nembutsu for the purpose of fulfilling his obligation of filial piety. What impact would a statement like that have in ancient and traditional Japan? What is the background of such a denial?

The roots of Shinran's teaching can be traced to the writings of Honen, his master, and Honen's disciples. They distinguished between the way of rebirth through various practices and the way of the sole practice of the Nembutsu, based on the Original Vow. Further, in the category of various practices, the Pure Land tradition distinguished two types of virtuous activities. One was the Buddhist discipline and system of meditations aiming at emancipation and enlightenment. The other included the whole range of moral deeds performed by ordinary people in society. The Confucian pattern of morality focusing upon loyalty (*chu*) and filial piety (*ko*) was central. Filial piety and obedience to the teacher and leader were the mainstays of social morality in the Pure Land tradition.

As the story of Buddha's renunciation of family and social life indicates, early Buddhism considered that the achievement of enlightenment was more important than the maintenance of social obligations. A monk was called "a homeless one" (*shukke*). Spiritual cultivation had the highest priority.

However, when Buddhism entered China, the Confucianists, who emphasized social obligation as the highest priority, seized upon this point to oppose the spread of Buddhism. They claimed Buddhism was socially irresponsible because it encouraged youth to forsake society and family to seek their own welfare.

Buddhism responded to the challenge by stressing the spiritual benefits it offered to society and the role the monk played in securing a blessed destiny for one's ancestors. Buddhism adapted to the Chinese concern for ancestors and family by developing ceremonies aimed at the welfare of the departed.

The Obon festival and the Higan ceremonies reveal how Buddhism solved the problem. The story of the monk Mogallana, which is the basis of the Obon celebration, tells how the monk Mogallana, after he had gained Buddhist insight, discovered the suffering of his mother as a hungry ghost. Through Buddhism, he was able to release her from her miseries. Confucianism could not do this because it was concerned only with worldly morality and human relations.

In the *Kyogyoshinsho* Shinran quotes a section from a Chinese text: *Benshoron*, which attempted to answer widespread criticisms of Buddhism that in contrast to the Taoist sage Lao-tzu's service to society, Shakyamuni abandoned his parents and social obligations.[1] Such stringent criticism caused Buddhism to conform more and more to the demands of Chinese, and, later, Japanese society. Kamakura Buddhists such as Honen, Shinran, Dogen, and Nichiren tried to restore Buddhism to its original and pure spirit in relation to society. That is, they claimed that spiritual priorities were more basic than social demands. Dogen retired to Fukui, refusing to go to Kamakura, while Honen, Shinran, and Nichiren were persecuted for their views.

Pure Land Buddhism, before the time of Honen and Shinran, generally emphasized achieving salvation in the other world or afterlife. It was considered an otherworldly religion. However, it became a leader in the struggle against folk traditions which exploited and created anxiety among the people. The consoling teaching of Honen and Shinran was a liberating teaching at the time, although the liberation it offered resulted in continual persecution. Shinran, in the volume on *Transformed Buddha and Transformed Land* in the *Kyogyoshinsho*, comments sharply on the error of folk beliefs. He quotes numerous Buddhist texts which clearly rejected superstitions. A significant quote now under much discussion in Japan came from the *Bosatsukaikyo* (Sutra of Bodhisattva Precepts), which declared that followers of Buddha do not bow before kings or revere parents or demons.

Shinran also quoted from the *Benshoron* the Buddhist view of social relations in answer to the Chinese criticism:

> A Buddhist Sutra states that the roots of conscious-
> ness transmigrate through the six paths. There are
> none (who at sometime) are not father or mother.
> Transforming through the three worlds of birth and
> death, who will distinguish enemy or friend? It also
> states that while they still travel through birth and
> death and commit acts in their comings and goings
> because ignorance covers the eyes of wisdom,
> (beings) are mutually fathers and sons and acquaint-
> ances are often friends or enemies while enemies
> and friends are often acquaintances. Therefore the
> monk abandons secular life and betakes himself to
> the truth.[2]

Clearly, this is the basis for Shinran's statement that he has never once said the Nembutsu for his own parents, a state-ment in which he makes real in his own life and teachings the Buddhist universalism that transcends all social, racial, polit-ical, and cultural barriers. We are all one. The respect that we owe our immediate parents and kin, we also owe equally to all beings. Major teachings of Buddhist philosophy emphasize this view whether it be the intersecting karmic destinies, the law of interdependence, or the universal Buddha in all beings. There is an essential oneness to which our egoistic delusions blind us.

Shinran went further than the traditional Buddhism of his time in stressing that though we might desire to do so, we cannot save others by our self-effort. As he showed in the chapter concerning the sage path compassion and Pure Land compassion, final salvation can only result from the work of Amida Buddha. Our hope is to become a Buddha, united with universal, all-embracing compassion.

It is important to see the relation between the two reasons Shinran advances for rejecting the Nembutsu of filial piety. The universal ideal could be followed in a self-powered way, as is done in many Buddhist ceremonies in the transfer of merit for all spirits in the three worlds. Shinran is saying that we must keep in our mind our human limits in striving for ultimate goals. Only in this way can we avoid the pride and presumption that we cultivate in acts of piety. He is also pointing out that the goal of religion lies in saving others. We can share in that goal when we have attained Buddhahood. For Shinran, the ultimate way of respect for parents is not the limited religious act of transferring merit of a good deed, but the development of deep faith and the universal compassion that is the true source of salvation and leads to Buddhahood.

CHAPTER **10**

Shinran's Social Awareness

In chapter six of the *Tannisho*, Shinran makes a highly paradoxical statement that has become one of his most remembered phrases: "I, Shinran, have not even a single disciple." This declaration, just as in the instance of the rejection of Buddhist practices of filial piety, reveals Shinran's personal denial of using the Confucian perspective in human relations under the cover of Buddhism, as had been the accommodation of Buddhists in China and in Shinran's own homeland, Japan.

Shinran particularly repudiated the Confucian social class discrimination which subordinated the so-called "inferior" person to the "superior" person in the five relationships of ruler and subject, parents and children, older and younger sibling, husband and wife, teacher and disciple. In stunning contrast to this, Shinran maintained that the authoritarian society based on class and status had no place in true Buddhism. We can find clear evidence of this not only in Shinran's personal relations with his disciples but even in his language, where he employed honorific terms in addressing his followers. Though they were peasants, farmers, illiterate, uneducated, he never spoke to them in a demeaning fashion, nor with a dogmatic spirit, but as fellow beings of equal blindness, equal foolishness, and similar suffering.

Shinran's assertion that he had no disciples must have made a great impression upon the early community, an impression discussed in *Kudensho 6* and *Gaijasho 4* as well as in the writings of Rennyo Shonin. The passage in *Kudensho* relates the incident that gave rise to Shinran's declaration. When he was in Kyoto with some other followers, one Shingyo-bo separated himself from the fellowship on some disagreement and returned to Kanto. Other disciples urged Shinran to take back the object of worship and signed texts that he had given Shingyo-bo as his authority to represent Shin teaching, but Shinran refused to do this on the ground that he did not create faith. It was, he told them, not his property, and it was at this point he made the statement that he does not really have disciples. This is a statement that, as Professor Masutani Fumio has indicated in his writings, is unique in religious history. Only Socrates and St. Paul have made similar declarations. Socrates regarded his followers as equals when he engaged in dialogue. In Christianity, St. Paul was unique in rejecting sectarianism and parties by claiming that it is only God who saves, and therefore Paul himself has no disciples.

The term used by Shinran to refer to his associates was *ondobo* (fellow followers) or *ondogyo* (fellow practicers of the faith). These words reflect Shinran's democratic ideal of human relations flowing from the meaning of Amida's Vows. These were not terms invented by Shinran, but were earlier employed in Zendo's writings as well as the Tendai *Makashikan* of China. In Zendo's *Hojisan* such words were used to refer to people who are identified by common aspiration and endeavors. In the *Makashikan* they refer to three types of good friends. Rennyo Shonin wrote in his letters that Shinran declared he had no disciples, referring to his followers as *ondobo* or *ondogyo*, and this is why members of Shinshu call each other *dobo* or *dogyo*. It was erroneous in Shinshu to call a person *deshi* (disciple) because such a term implied inferior status.

In our modern contemporary world, Shinran's principle has great importance for religion and education. It can be productively related to a new focus on the relationships between students and faculty, layman and clergy. If, as Shinran states, there is "neither priest nor layman" (*hiso hizoku*), then there can in fact be neither teacher nor disciple. The problem in contemporary education is the lack of mutuality between the student and the teacher. We have entirely lost the sense that we are all engaged in a common enterprise of learning and entering into truth, that it is a shared endeavor. In most religious and educational institutions the teacher is regarded as an authority, and the lay person does not feel responsible for cultivating his own insight and sharing it. The teacher is expected to give and the student to receive.

In recent years there have been many movements and methods which have attempted to remedy the situation with group dynamics or sensitivity training. Through the use of psychological technique, many have been able to transcend the boundaries of personality, sex, and status, to share their life with others. However, in Shinran we discover a philosophical and religious basis for achieving the sense of identity and mutuality which are necessary to real learning and truly ethical living.

Shinran, through his marriage, his family life, and his experience of sharing the difficulties of life in ordinary society, broke down the barriers of status and prestige that attend religious figures. Even in his pictures, he is portrayed wearing a layman's, not a clerical, dress. While the intervening centuries since his lifetime have elevated him in the eyes of his followers so that he is now commonly referred to as "Saint Shinran," this was never Shinran's way nor desire.

In his ethical and personal principles Shinran avoided authoritarian and externally imposed standards of conduct. He desired people to develop their inner life on the basis of faith. When moral and ethical problems appeared in his community, he urged his followers to consider their acts and not turn their freedom into license. His principle was that we should not take a poison merely because there is an antidote. As illustration of his appeal to inner commitment, we can observe at the end of chapter six of the *Tannisho* his statement that when we are aware of the natural principle of things, gratitude to the Buddha and teachers will spontaneously arise. He is saying that respect and responsiveness to a teacher cannot be demanded, but only truly arises from the perception of the good one has received from others. When we understand deeply how much others contribute to our lives, we will naturally become grateful.

In relation to contemporary ethical thought, Shinran's outlook can be supported by, and correlated with, the theory of situational ethics developed by the Episcopal theologian Joseph Fletcher. He rejected all objectivistic, legalistic moralities sanctioned by communal or traditional authoritarian religious prescriptions. He replaced them by an inwardly generated sensitivity to the needs of the other, based on love and compassion. While there are many problems in the application of this theory to modern society, it has the virtue of reducing the judgmental attitude of people by allowing a person to follow his conscience; and it reduces hypocrisy, the bane of all religion, by encouraging people to follow the norms of their own conscience rather than merely conform to an external code. It calls for integration of the person and cultivation of deep faith.

The structure of the religious life that we perceive in Shinran's teaching is significant for its denial of legalism and moralism, and for its attempt to base life on the deep inward awareness of finitude—our own imperfections—and gratitude. Shinran's religious philosophy has been termed the religion beyond good and evil. It is an apt description when we understand that by giving up the conscious, moralistic distinctions of good and evil as the means of comparing ourselves with others (a means whereby the comparison is usually favorable to ourselves), religion becomes an influence to unite people rather than a barrier to separate and judge people. In this way, the single-mindedness of faith will flow into the oneness of the community, inspired by the compassion which embraces and never rejects.

CHAPTER **11**

The Way of No-Hindrance

In four simple statements, chapter seven of the *Tannisho* describes the spiritual status of the Nembutsu devotee.

> The follower of the Nembutsu treads the unobstructed Single Path. If we ask the reason why, it is because even the gods of heaven and earth reverence and bow to the devotee who has true faith, and the evil spirits and those of false ways never hinder. Sins and evil cannot result in karmic retribution. Because good deeds never surpass the Nembutsu, it is the unobstructed Single Path.

Chapters, four, five, and six of the *Tannisho*, view the Nembutsu in relation to other people and in reference to practices of compassion, filial piety, or relations with disciples and fellow devotees. The subject matter of these chapters is externally oriented. However, chapters seven, eight, and nine look inward to the way of life and attitude as well as to the spiritual status of the person of true faith.

Chapter seven is a terse and profound declaration of the ultimate status of the believer. Just how ultimate or absolute is that condition? We must first observe the meaning of the first statement in the chapter, that "the follower of the Nembutsu treads the unobstructed Single Path," a phrase which refers to the final attainment of Buddhahood. The use of this phrase may be traced back to the *Kegon Sutra*, which Shinran quotes in the *Kyogyoshinsho*:

> Those who bear no impediments transcend birth-and-death by means of the One Way.[1]

This idea was treated in more detail in the Chinese patriarch Donran's commentary on the *Pure Land Treatise* of Vasubandhu:

> The Enlightenment (or Way) is the Way of no hindrance. According to a Sutra (the *Kegon Sutra*) a man of no-hindrance transcends birth-and-death by means of the One Way. The One Way is no other than the way of no-hindrance, and the way of no-hindrance is to know that birth-and-death is Nirvana itself ...[2]

The important thing to note here is that Shinran applies to persons of faith the qualifications that Mahayana Buddhism employed to define the attainment of Buddhahood. This is a singular feature of Shinran's teaching which stands in sharp contrast to other forms of Buddhism. Shinran's view is that in the very moment when faith arises, one's ultimate destiny becomes absolutely and irrevocably assured. Therefore he describes the believer's situation as having entered the *Assembly of the Truly Assured*. This term, in early Mahayana Buddhism, merely referred to a stage in the Bodhisattva's progress to Buddhahood. In Pure Land teaching before Shinran, it was a state of Non-Retrogression. According to Shinran, this condition is not a matter of ages of discipline in the Bodhisattva path, nor a consequence of future birth into the Pure Land, but a present condition realized at the very moment faith arises in the mind and heart.

Another way that Shinran describes this condition is to say that people of faith are *Equal to the Tathagata*, that is, equal to the Buddha. He writes to a disciple:

> Because people who have attained faith surely abide in the Assembly of the Truly Assured, we say that it is the status (or rank) equivalent to enlightenment ...

> The (ideas of) the Assembly of the Truly Assured and
> Equal to Enlightenment have the same meaning and
> the same status.[3]

The basis for Shinran's teaching was his firm faith that salvation does not depend on the fitful, erratic, egoistic, or self-righteous actions by which people strive to acquire merit and spiritual power. Rather, salvation is entirely the result of Amida's compassion expressed in the Original Vow to save all beings. A related term which is important for Shinran is *"the embrace which does not reject."* Salvation comes from Amida's embrace, gathering, or taking in. It is not the result of human efforts.

The religious symbols and principles behind Shinran's Buddhology worked a transformation in the hearts of his followers. He gave them a basis in Buddhist thought and a confidence that, despite misfortunes and mistakes that arise in our lives, our destinies are sealed forever. Though the future is unknown and we always fear the future, we do not have the added anxiety that we might fall into evil destinies and sufferings after this life. Popular Buddhism since earliest times held up pictures of frightful consequences of sin in order to arouse righteous behavior.

The practical consequence of Shinran's teaching was a rejection of the ancient practice of deathbed ceremonies designed to ensure birth in the Pure Land. Thus he wrote:

> The person who has attained true faith abides in the
> Assembly of the Truly Assured on account of the
> Embrace which does not reject. Therefore, there
> is no waiting for the last moment, no depending
> on the Buddha's coming to meet. When faith is
> determined, rebirth into the Pure Land is also deter-
> mined. One does not wait on the ceremonies of the
> Buddha's meeting (at the point of death).[4]

Although Shinran employs abstract and philosophical thought, we must not underestimate the liberating impact his message conveyed to his disciples, a message which they surely understood.

Life is filled with anxieties and uncertainties. People's limited knowledge and power lead them always to attempt to unravel the future or cultivate some power that gives them control over the circumstances of their lives. Hence the perennial interest in divination and the occult that even pervades our own sophisticated age. Shinran, however, clearly believed that religion and faith should illumine the realities of life and abolish unnecessary anxieties and fears. In this he was following the example and spirit of Shakyamuni Buddha, who helped the people of his time to accept the reality of Impermanence.

Shinran, as did Shakyamuni Buddha, rejected superstitious belief and practices which traded on fear. Both Shinran and Shakyamuni Buddha regarded religion as a source of spiritual liberation and emancipation, rather than a way to control people through fear. For Shinran, religion was a power for living. He transformed the traditional Pure Land teaching, which focused on the afterlife, to a way of living positively and meaningfully in this world with oneself and with one's companions in life and faith.

The Benefits of Faith

In the *Tannisho*, chapter seven, Shinran declares that the person of true faith instantaneously receives status equivalent to enlightenment—or to Buddhahood—because Amida Buddha includes the individual in his embrace which does not reject. In other words, the final destiny of the believer has been determined and guaranteed by the fulfillment of Amida's Vow.

The psychological implications of this teaching in relieving anxiety about present and future life are manifest. In addition, Shinran outlined several spiritual benefits which come to the person of faith. These are, first, that the gods of heaven and earth revere and bow to the devotee; second, that evil spirits or false teachers and teachings cannot deter the believer; and third, that evil deeds or sins do not incur karmic retribution. Shinran concluded that all these blessings came about because faith expressed through the Nembutsu is the supreme good, as in chapter four it was the final compassion. Each of these blessings of faith has, in addition to spiritual and practical significance, the function of becoming a foundation in the meaning of Buddhahood, to which level the believer has now been spiritually elevated.

For the ancient world, Shinran's assertion that the gods of heaven and earth revere the believer was indeed bold. Yet, its root is to be found in the fact that when Gautama attained enlightenment, the gods of the universe came to honor him and became his followers. Thus there is a basis in Buddhist myth for Shinran's teaching, and he could apply it to people of faith since they have been raised to the status of equality with Buddha.

On the practical side, this assertion has great significance for the character of religion. Through the ages, in all countries and cultures, including Japan, people have been dominated by their fear of gods. They have bowed before the gods in order to avoid their anger. Many people therefore claim that religion is rooted only in fear, and as such is an obstacle to human development.

Whether it is high or low forms of religion, there is, of course, much evidence for this claim. Shinran, however, saw that the depth of Amida's compassion overwhelmed any threat which gods might pose to people of faith. His teaching was like that of Shakyamuni, who also taught that people need not fear gods, who held high the value of the dignity of the human person, and who claimed as human potential the highest spiritual achievement, even beyond the gods.

This recognition of the superiority of humanity over the gods in faith permits the believer to concentrate devotion to Amida without needing to appeal to other divinities to assist in human affairs. What this makes possible is the integration of human personality and life. It signifies giving direction to life in pursuit of the highest values of compassion and wisdom as symbolized in Amida Buddha. Early Shinshu followers were called *Ikko* followers because in the foregoing way they single-mindedly revered and worshipped Amida Buddha.

The second benefit, that in which the evil spirits and opponents of Buddhism are unable to deter the person of faith, likewise has its basis in Buddha myth. When Gautama was practicing and meditating in the quest of enlightenment, Mara, the Buddhist Satan, tried to tempt him away from his goal. Later, many stories tell of the persecutions and troubles which Buddha encountered. Some texts contain prophecies of Shakyamuni Buddha where he describes the troubles his followers will meet in later times.

When Shinran says that evil spirits and false teachers and teachings cannot deter the believer, he does not mean that we will not have problems or that life will be easy. Rather, like Shakyamuni, he means that despite all problems and regardless of how difficult our lives may seem, we will not be turned away from our destiny.

Two things usually inhibit wholehearted and deep involvement in religion today. These are, first, the attractions of ordinary pleasures and diversions and, second, opposition. The modern believer may not experience temptation directly from Mara or endure such persecution as Shakyamuni is reputed to have had or Shinran experienced. In our time, the evils that Buddhist sutras describe as Mara are represented by the easy excuses that people make for not taking up the study of religion, and for not participating in religion. When we substitute lesser values for the supreme values of compassion and wisdom, we are experiencing and succumbing to the reality of Mara the tempter. When we experience ridicule or suspicion because we involve our lives in religion, we are indeed experiencing opposition. Nevertheless, Shinran declares that these cannot obstruct people of true faith, because the root and inspiration of their faith is in the Vow of Amida. Ultimately the power of faith will win through over those obstacles which attempt to undermine and weaken us.

On the popular level, we may also note that Shinran here abolishes concern for folk beliefs. The derangements and problems brought about by fear of demons and evil spirits are wiped away through the realization that Amida's embrace and compassion protects the believer from such powers. It is psychological fact that people are bothered by such phenomena if they have the predisposition to it. If their consciousness is focused on Amida, no such problems can arise. Sound faith is a precondition of mental health.

The third benefit is perhaps the most significant of all the implications of Amida's embrace. People of faith no longer need to worry about karmic retribution. This fact is also based on the concept of Buddhahood behind Shinran's teaching.

Buddha, through his enlightenment, transcended and broke the bondage to the stream of birth and death and thus the karmic cycle. He was emancipated.

Shinran was a realist. He was not saying that we are actually Buddhas in this life. We are still passion-ridden human beings. We commit sins and make errors. Shinran, as a Buddhist, believed in the principle of cause and effect which is the basis of karma and central to Buddhism. He recognized that our acts have consequences on many levels of life. Thus we must understand him carefully.

In the area of spiritual reality, Shinran emphasizes that Amida's compassion is the ultimate cause and basis of salvation. The realization or fulfillment of Amida's Vows cannot be limited by our good or evil deeds. Amida's way is supreme over all, as Shinran notes in chapter one of the *Tannisho*. The embrace which does not reject is the foundation of our final attainment. That foundation is not merely the limited deeds which we perform, for though our deeds may have effect in our lives and in our relations, they do not determine our ultimate destiny. Thus, Shinran's revolutionary religious message: we do not buy salvation with good deeds or lose it through evil deeds.

Rather than attempting to purge evil and repress our passions, Shinran advocates relying more on Amida. Through the Nembutsu we can become more deeply and gratefully aware of the compassion that embraces our lives. In this way, chapter seven of the *Tannisho* offers liberation and hope to people filled with fears. There is no blind submission to evil or yielding to fear, but a joyous recognition of the deeper spiritual resources that can inspire courage and confidence in facing the difficulties of life.

The Revolutionary Reality of the Nembutsu

The spiritual status and attitudes of the devotee are set forth in the unique way of Shinran in chapters seven, eight, and nine of the *Tannisho*. Chapter seven, which elaborated the benefits the individual receives from the Nembutsu, had to be followed by chapter eight—which clarifies just what the Nembutsu itself is from which the blessings derive. In this clarification, Shinran declares firmly that the Nembutsu is neither a practice nor a good deed or virtue. The Nembutsu, furthermore, is not something a person does to gain benefits or to qualify for salvation.

By Shinran's day, eight hundred years ago, the term Nembutsu had a long history in Buddhism as a mode of meditating on the Buddha and cultivating in oneself the way to enlightenment and Buddhahood. In that long history, the term Nembutsu was first applied to the recitation of a Buddha's name, and finally came to mean the recitation of the Name of Amida Buddha as a way to purify oneself from ages of karmic corruption and to gain merit toward birth in the Pure Land. The exclusion of all practices other than that of the recitation of Amida's Name came to be the central teaching of Shinran's teacher, Honen. Shinran later distinguished himself from other followers of Honen by maintaining that the Nembutsu is not a means to salvation, but is the sign of salvation already experienced. Therefore, Shinran's unique contribution, a new direction in Pure Land Buddhism—indeed a new direction in religious thought—came out of his statement, as repeated by Yuien-bo in chapter eight, that the Nembutsu is neither a practice nor a good deed.

In Buddhism, the term practice—or discipline—refers to the system of meditations and precepts by which monks prepared themselves for enlightenment. In Buddhist tradition there were four stages through which a devotee would pass in the Theravada teachings, four subdivisions of spiritual experience leading to Nirvana. In Mahayana Buddhism there are described ten stages of the Bodhisattva path and fifty-three stages set forth in the *Kegon Sutra.* Thus to undertake practice in Buddhism requires a tremendous inner commitment to attain enlightenment, and the unflagging resolve of the seeker to persist through a long process. For those who seriously entered either path, it was a heroic endeavor.

Moral deeds, or the cultivation of good roots, have always been the essential foundation of Buddhism. The initial five precepts which relate to one's behavior in the world cultivate these good roots by not lying, stealing, killing, drinking excessively, or engaging in unchastity. The *Dhammapada*, an ancient Buddhist text, is highly ethical in content. Along with mental attitudes conducive to enlightenment, the divisions of the Eightfold Noble Path involve proper ethical and social behavior. The centrality of ethics in Buddhist teaching was observed and stressed by early western scholars of Buddhism, whose contact was mainly with Theravada, or traditional Mahayana, either the path of four stages or that of the ten stage Bodhisattva path and the fifty-three stages set forth in the *Kegon Sutra.*

Yet Shinran declares that the Nembutsu is neither of these two facets of Buddhist life and behavior. How could he do this? Shinran had both his own experience of serious discipline on Mt. Hiei and the teaching of Amida's Vows (the ultimate foundation of salvation), to support him. From the standpoint of his own experience, Shinran had spent twenty years on

Mt. Hiei engaged in the struggle to advance toward enlightenment. However, by his own testimony the strength of his ego
and passions prevented him. He was able to perceive the deeper
egoism resulting from the pursuit of such goals as, under the
cover of religious faith, people competed for fame and power.

Shinran recognized that all religious efforts that appeal to
the individual's self-interest in order to gain salvation only
reinforce the egoism which Buddhism declares is the source of
suffering and from which we must be rescued. To appeal to ego
to save ego is self-contradictory. No one before Shinran had
ever offered this radical perception.

If this egoistic self-contradiction had been all Shinran
perceived in religious discipline, he would have given up in
despair. However, he came to realize that the Vows of Amida
Buddha provided the way out of the spiritual dilemma he
faced. Both as a disciple of Honen and, later, as he worked
among the people, Shinran probed the meaning of Amida's
Vows and came to realize that salvation in every aspect is
derived from Amida's compassionate intention. We can take
no credit for the salvation that we share and that we become
assured of in the moment of faith. It is given to us without
regard to our accumulated merit from good deeds or our
practice of self-effort, and therefore his statement in chapter
eight sounds a revolution in religious thought.

Shinran follows his declaration with the further statement
that the Nembutsu is not a practice or a good deed done by our
own design or according to our own intention. He constantly
rejects the aspect of *hakarai* which accompanies human actions.
Hakarai refers to conscious and deliberate calculating that
goes with our actions. In the case of human *hakarai*, there is the
intention to pursue one's own good. Since he also uses the
term to refer to Amida's intention, the difference lies in the
fact that Amida gave himself solely to the benefit of others,
refusing to accept the fruits of enlightenment unless all others
could share it with him.

An example of the expression human *hakarai* from Pure
Land tradition may be seen in the biographies of famous

monks, where they are reputed to have recited the Nembutsu fifty or sixty thousand times a day. Before Shinran, the *quantity* of Nembutsu was the distinguishing feature. With Shinran, an emphasis on the *attitude* and *spirit* with which one recites Nembutsu becomes central. He concludes the passage in chapter eight of the *Tannisho* by noting that when we seriously understand the meaning of Other Power and have left off our self-power attitudes, we will understand why the Nembutsu is non-practice and non-good.

The point of the passage is not to dissuade his followers from reciting the Nembutsu, but to have them understand its true source and the real basis of the benefits they receive from it. Shinran was a realist in spiritual matters. He understood that refraining from acting, as well as performing acts, may stimulate the ego to pride and competition on the relative level. How many religious people are proud of what they don't do? The real problem of religion is not the deeds, but the inner attitudes of people who perform the deeds.

Shinran attempts to transform our understanding of the meaning of religious actions. Only those acts which arise spontaneously in response to the awareness of being embraced in Amida's compassion (that is, out of gratitude) have any religious meaning. The source of even these acts are to be found in Amida. We must act, but we can take no credit for the act.

Shinran's teaching has sometimes been criticized for claiming that a person need do nothing in order to be saved. Thus Shin Buddhism has been called a do-nothing religion. When this criticism is properly understood, it becomes a compliment to his profound insight because he removed from religion all basis for hypocrisy. He removed all obligatory aspects of religion which encourage people to pose as religious when their heart is not really in it. Shinran never required anyone to prove that he was saved. He never specified when, how, or how many Nembutsu were required.

He did believe that a deep awareness of the reality of the Vow would evoke a response of Nembutsu. Thus he declared:

... although the one moment of shinjin and the one moment of nembutsu are two, there is no nembutsu separate from shinjin, nor is the one moment of shinjin separate from the one moment of nembutsu.... Both should be understood to be Amida's Vow. Nembutsu and shinjin on our part are themselves the manifestations of the Vow.[1]

Contained in these words of Shinran is a spiritual revolution where, in every area of life, spirit triumphs over form.

The Affirmation of Doubt

The *Tannisho* chapter nine is a remarkable passage. In it we gain insight both into the nature of the Nembutsu experience, and the manner in which Shinran dealt with the spiritual problems of his disciples and companions. It is in this chapter that Yuien-bo tells us how he came to Shinran perplexed and concerned because he did not experience joy in his faith nor did he desire to go to the Pure Land. Yuien-bo naturally wondered if, this being his true feeling, he was really saved.

Immediately Shinran calms his fears by indicating that he, Shinran himself, has had the same doubts and anxieties, but that he has come to realize such anxieties are signs that salvation is secure, since Amida in his great compassion already understands and provides for these human dilemmas that result from our ineradicable passions. In this discussion with Yuien-bo, Shinran reveals astute insight into religious psychology as he draws positive philosophical principles from negative experiences.

The moment Yuien-bo confessed his doubts and anxieties, Shinran identified himself with Yuien-bo by declaring, "I, Shinran, have also had this doubt." Shinran did not assume a superior position and chide Yuien-bo for his lack of proper faith. Rather, he took Yuien-bo's burden upon himself and proceeded to show how to resolve the problem. In the resolution, Shinran did not demand Yuien-bo purge himself of these doubts. Rather, he attempted to have Yuien-bo understand why they arise and that they are natural to our human condition. In this way, Shinran acted to restore Yuien-bo's self-confidence through positive acceptance, demonstrating a profoundly realistic insight into human nature. He was able to show Yuien-bo that he was not alone in his dilemma, and that the existence of the problem in no way threatened his ultimate salvation. Instead, it was a sign of the certainty of his salvation.

Here Shinran clearly understood that the ideal of religion may be freedom from doubt; but in our finite, limited, and passionate lives, how can we attain that ideal? It is for this reason that Amida makes the evil person the object of his salvation. Shinran's compassionate embrace of Yuien-bo is a dramatic portrayal of the meaning of Amida's compassion as depicted in the sutra. The impact of Shinran's compassionate character, as exemplified in chapter nine's resolution of Yuien-bo's dilemma concerning his faith, led Eshinni (Shinran's wife), and many of Shinran's followers to regard him as a veritable embodiment of Amida in this world. It is in such a fashion that the reality of any religious symbol depends on its expression and fulfillment in human life.

Chapter nine thus deals with fundamental religious issues. All religions proclaiming salvation assert that, at the prospect of ultimate release, faith expresses itself in joy. Even the *Larger Pure Land Sutra* declares that all gods and people in the ten worlds, "upon hearing my name, prostrate themselves on the ground to worship me in joy and trust, and practice the Bodhisattva discipline ..."[1] Yet the recurring problem is that, despite strong belief, it is difficult to be joyous all the time. Since our feelings are unstable, if the awareness of joy is turned into a criterion of salvation or a requirement to prove one's salvation, a deep dilemma is created. Because he could not produce the feelings of joy he thought were supposed to be evidence of salvation, Yuien-bo came to doubt his salvation.

His second dilemma was that though he believed in the Pure Land as his ultimate destiny, he did not wish to go there quickly. It is a fact that people desire to live as long as possible, despite their belief that they will go to heaven. As Shinran himself notes, we continue to cling to our lives of suffering and do not desire to go to the Pure Land in which we have never been born and which we do not know. Despite beliefs in the afterlife and glorious pictures of it given by religion, the fear of the unknown and attachment to the pleasures we experience in life overwhelm our supposed belief in paradise.

Shinran's identification with Yuien-bo in his dilemmas was not a mere pose. He declares in the *Kyogyoshinsho*:

> Truly I know. Sad it is that I, Gutoku Ran, sunk in the vast sea of lust and lost in the great mountain of desire for fame and profit, do not rejoice in joining the group of the Rightly Established State, nor do I enjoy coming near to the True Enlightenment. What a shame! What a sorrow![2]

Shinran heightens the paradox by speaking much about faith and joy in the volume on *Faith* in the *Kyogyoshinsho*. "The benefit of having much joy in mind" is one of the ten benefits resulting from faith. He also states: "The Great Joyful Mind is the True Faith." And, further,

> As I contemplate the True Serene Faith, there is one thought in the Serene Faith. "One thought" reveals the moment of the first thought of the awakened Serene Faith and it expresses the great and inconceivable Joyful Mind.[3]

Shinran experienced joy in his faith but, without any diminution of that total faith, he also suffered from lack of joy. What he is indicating for us, then, is the joy of the moment when one first becomes aware of the truth of Amida's compassion. It is the joy that comes with conversion or in other flickering moments when one becomes aware of the depth of meaning of the Buddha Dharma. That we are unable to maintain the intensity of those moments of deep insight and realization is because of the continued power of the passions which hang over our minds as clouds cover the sun or moon and obscure the brilliance of their light. In our general experience, the romance and love of courtship differs in intensity and freshness from married love because of the cares and busyness and routine that beset family life. First moments can rarely be repeated.

Shinran resolves the dilemma for himself and Yuien-bo, as well as for ourselves, by stressing that awareness of the gap between the realities of our lives and the ideals of faith is the result of Amida's compassion illuminating our lives and thereby assuring our salvation.

This is an astute psychological observation. In effect, Shinran is telling us, awareness of our imperfection and inability even to express the ideals of faith, despite our belief, is the basis of the humility and egolessness that is the way of salvation in Buddhism. The psychological implications of Shinran's approach have recently been developed in a practical way in the Naikan form of psychotherapy in Japan. This is a method which employs guilt in a positive fashion to bring about rehabilitation. According to Takao Murase:

> Naikan therapy is based upon the philosophy that the human being is fundamentally selfish and guilty, yet at the same time favored with unmeasured benevolence from others. In order to acknowledge these existential conditions deeply, one must become open-minded towards oneself, empathetic and sympathetic toward others, and must courageously confront his own authentic guilt. Only then will he achieve new identity.[4]

In chapter nine, in his resolution of Yuien-bo's problem, Shinran gave practical expression to the doctrine of two types of deep faith, a basic teaching of Pure Land tradition since the time of Zendo in China. According to this teaching, awareness of evil and imperfection in ourselves, and the illumination of our lives by Amida, are two sides or aspects of the same situation. When our lives are viewed from the standpoint of the perfection of compassion and purity in Amida, we become aware of our own limitations.

Recently, during a demonstration of a vacuum cleaner, the salesman turned on a bright light which revealed how much dust was in the air, a condition generally unseen by the naked eye. As the intense light highlighted the dust, so the light of Amida reveals the true nature of our lives. Thus Shinran's conclusion in his counsel to Yuien-bo that since our awareness of evil is the result of Amida's compassionate activity in our minds, the more unworthy and uncertain we feel about our salvation, the more we can be assured of being embraced by Amida.

CHAPTER **15**

The Basis of True Salvation

Chapter ten of the *Tannisho* is, perhaps, the shortest chapter of any book in the world. In its entirety, it states:

> The master said, "The meaning of the Nembutsu is that it is beyond all logic. For it is beyond calculation, beyond explanation, and beyond understanding (*Nembutsu ni wa Mugi o motte Gi to su. Fukasho, fukasetsu, fukashigi no yue ni to ose soraiki*)."

No translation yet available in English quite conveys the essence of the original Japanese. In Japanese, the term *gi* has such a wide range of meaning. These include: logic, principle, meaning, reason, trait, function, benefit. When Shinran analyzes the word, he interprets it as *hakarai*, which generally means calculation, contrivance, deliberation, discrimination, and measure. *Hakarai* has the nuance of self-will or self-assertion. It is identified in Pure Land terminology with self-power. Thus the word has intellectual aspects as well as attitudinal dimensions.

In this concluding statement of the first section of the *Tannisho*, Shinran is suggesting that, despite all the words that one may use to explain and make clear the meaning of the Nembutsu and Amida's Vow, ultimately it is a paradox and great mystery. Interestingly, Yuien-bo puts this statement at the end rather than the beginning. He does not use mystery as a way of avoiding discussion or inhibiting questions. It comes as the conclusion of the matter, when we have probed as deeply as we can. In this sense, chapter ten reflects intellectual and spiritual humility.

The mystery that eludes words is the compassion of Amida Buddha, which reaches out to embrace even the most desperate sinner. It is the mystery of the Vow itself, which symbolizes not only the universality of Buddha's compassion, but its indivisibility. The Vow declares that even though he were to become Buddha, Amida would not accept the highest enlightenment unless all other beings could attain it with him. In effect, salvation is only complete when all receive it. The sutra declares that the Vow has been fulfilled. Therefore, in effect, Shinran's interpretation is that all are saved, though they may not be aware of it in their finite conscious experience.

The scope, the depth, the richness, the wonder, the hope and joy of such compassion eludes the capacity of finite minds to conceive or express adequately. We cannot exhaust its meaning. Approaching it, as Yuien-bo's single statement of chapter ten, our words are only flickering lights in a vast darkness.

While, intellectually, the statement "the meaning of the Nembutsu is that it is beyond all logic" indicates a reason that lies beyond reason, attitudinally it is applied by Shinran to the mind of faith in Amida Buddha and to the rejection of self-will. The phrase means to give up calculation and deliberation in attempting to gain assurance of salvation. So, for Shinran, the Nembutsu is an uncalculated and spontaneous act.

Undoubtedly, Shinran was aware that some people recited the Nembutsu as a means of gaining salvation. Such people believed that each Nembutsu yielded merit that would purify from sin and qualify them for birth into the Pure Land. Shinran indicates that in reality the Nembutsu of true faith involves no such intention or calculation.

As an expression of Amida's limitless compassion in our consciousness, it is a profound mystery. The Nembutsu is not the means of salvation, but the witness or evidence of it. Its appearance is testimony that the Vow has actually been fulfilled.

Shinran's conception of the Nembutsu represents a revolution in religious understanding. According to him, all religious activity which is not inspired by deep faith in Amida's Vow is essentially self-willed religion. In such cases, people pursue religion out of self-interest and self-concern. They intend to gain salvation. This is the reasoning attitude which believes that quantity is quality.

In religions which advocate the cultivation of merit, there is the belief that the more virtue or merit one acquires, the closer one is to salvation. In ancient Pure Land tradition, the number of Nembutsu recited each day became the measure of sainthood. In some cases, it was believed that the louder one recited the Nembutsu, the larger the Buddha one would perceive.

For Shinran, just as faith is contrary to human expectations in the salvation of the evil person, so in the sphere of religious life religion is to be without purpose or intention. Religion serves no purpose—when purpose is understood as a personal benefit or self-advancement or becomes a vested interest. Religion for Shinran is not self-serving.

Shinran's radical perspective on religion can be roughly illustrated from observations of students. Students are generally more concerned with the requirements of a course. They want to know how much one must do to pass the course or succeed. They wish to know if an exam will be hard and what is its scope. They are usually more oriented to minimums than to maximums. They desire to know the least they can do for the maximum benefit. It is rare to find a student who is devoted to the learning process without calculating benefits.

Shinran realized that the calculation of benefits or aiming at the goal of salvation really increased egocentric tendencies within the person and ultimately blocked one's progress toward salvation. In our everyday experience we can observe this truth. The calculating person is easily detected. At work, the clock watcher reveals a half-hearted devotion to his work.

Those people who put aside, even in a small measure, their self-concern and throw themselves into their task, ultimately succeed. It is a fact of life that excessive ego-concern defeats the best interests of the self. In the same way, religion that focuses upon ego interest blocks the way to true ego-liberation because it stimulates pride, striving, calculation, and competition.

In the first ten chapters of the *Tannisho* there is a consistent and steady effort to illuminate the basis of true salvation through liberation from egoistic self-will. Beginning with the all-embracing, invincible character of the Original Vow, Yuien-bo traces a path from Shinran's declaration of the basic simplicity of faith and its basis in authority through the presentation of the evil person as the true object of Amida's compassion. Along the path of the *Tannisho*, section one, Yuien-bo gives consideration to Shinran's various aspects of the meaning of the Nembutsu. Shinran points out that the compassion of Buddha is limitless in comparison to finite human compassion and is universal, transcending clan and family, as well as the distinction between teacher and pupil. Thus he shows that in Shinran's teachings, the life of the Nembutsu is a path of freedom in the deepest sense, and is not based on the human distinctions of good and evil. Though we have doubts and anxieties, as Yuien-bo depicts himself as having, these are all signs of Buddha's compassion. Our salvation is absolutely assured. Everything points to an unspeakable mystery which goes beyond expression, yet is real in the faith it inspires and the liberation it offers.

Dealing with Differences

In the second section of the *Tannisho*, Yuien-bo attempts to clarify a variety of problems within the early Shinshu community. This section has its own preface, which is similar to that of the first section in that the reader's attention is directed to an awareness of lamentable misunderstandings and misinterpretations of Shinran's teachings. The two prefaces are different in both tone and specific content, though each helps us to gain a perspective on issues in dispute in the early community.

In the first preface, Yuien-bo collected words of Shinran that he remembered, and which were particularly relevant to the problems that arose among Shinran's followers after his death. There is a possibility that this first section of the *Tannisho* may well be the appendix to which Yuien-bo refers in his concluding epilogue, when he says: "I have selected some important passages and appended them to this book as a standard reference."

However, in view of the fact that the prefaces to the first section and to the second section introduce materials of a distinctly different character, it is possible that the second section was a separate text. Yuien-bo later appended the first section in order to strengthen his position in dealing with disputes.

The first section fits well the type of testimony or evidence Yuien-bo sought in Shinran's words. The ten succinct chapters of the first section also correlate well with the issues Yuien-bo takes up in the second section. The preface to the second section gives us more detail about the background of the disputes he addresses, and in it indicates that many people—young and old—had visited Shinran during his later years in Kyoto. They brought questions for him to solve (as we can observe in the *Tannisho*, chapter two). There they also asked whether Shinran had other teachings than those he had taught while in the Kanto area years before.

Despite the great effort many of his followers from those distant provinces made to visit Shinran in Kyoto, direct face-to-face contact did not prevent later misunderstanding and misinterpretations from arising. From his own background and experience with Shinran, Yuien-bo thus felt obligated to clarify the issues, since the master was no longer present to do so. This was undoubtedly a difficult task. Because of Yuien-bo's willingness and sense of obligation to do this, we now possess the *Tannisho*.

It is important to observe here that even during Shinran's lifetime, he had to deal with a multitude of problems. These appear scattered through those of his letters which deal with such issues as the nature of religious existence and practice, the last moment of life, moral behavior, and attitudes towards traditional religion and persecution. As an example, in *Mattosho* letters #16, #19, #20 and *Goshosokushu* #4, #5, #8, Shinran particularly refutes the idea that since Amida Buddha saves sinners unconditionally, it is all right to do evil as one wishes. This problem probably arose from Shinran's emphasis that despite the depth of sin and passion, Amida embraces even the most sinful person. To those who then misinterpreted his statement as a license for immoral behavior, Shinran declared that we should not take poison simply because there is an antidote for it.

Interestingly, a similar problem confronted the Apostle Paul in the New Testament. There he exclaimed: "God forbid that we should sin in order that grace may abound." In religions that provide salvation to sinful people, this problem occurs when the distinction between willfully motivated sin and that arising from passionate nature is not made clear.

When Shinran tried to deal with the various issues of misunderstanding of his teachings, the problems became so intense that he was forced even to disown his eldest son Zenran, who created more misunderstanding and division by claiming that he possessed secret teachings which Shinran had withheld from others.

The situation confronting Yuien-bo after Shinran's death has been repeated frequently in the history of religion. When the founder has passed from the scene, his statements—given in highly personal encounters and directed to certain issues—may well become the basis on which later followers build the interpretation of their faith. Vital spiritual exchange and counsel often become transformed into proposition and principle, which is then used as authority. The variety of statements may lead to a variety of viewpoints on what the founder actually meant. His words and works are collected and commentaries written in order to correlate and unify his teaching. In a way, Yuien-bo's *Tannisho* is an early commentary on Shinran's teaching.

Through Shinran's own writings, and those of Yuien-bo, we see that Shinran appears afflicted with controversies both during his lifetime and after. We may seek the reason for this in his freer style of leadership. Shinran did not impose a rigid adherence to his teachings and methods simply because he was the teacher. We have already seen in the *Tannisho*, chapter six, that he refused to excommunicate a follower, saying that the follower was not created by him or his teachings, but became a follower solely through Amida's embrace.

When the disciples came to Kyoto to seek his counsel, Shinran concluded: "Whether you entrust yourself to the Nembutsu or reject it is entirely up to you." We would say today that Shinran had an open personality. He had his firm convictions, but he was not coercive or imposing. His openness permitted more discussion of difference and was more accepting of difference. It was this personal openness that made Zenran's activities all the more embarrassing to Shinran. When

Zenran tried to enforce his father's authority over the disciples and they had to appeal to the father to discover whether this is what he desired, Shinran had no recourse but the painful one of disowning Zenran and all the authority that Zenran tried to claim for him.

Although difference and disagreement are generally considered undesirable in any group, both have a function in the life of a community—the function of clarifying and bringing to light the true meaning of the teaching on which that community is based.

This is true in Shinran's case because he delegated authority to his disciples when he left Kanto to return to Kyoto and because, as we have indicated, he had a more open personality. Rather than demanding loyalty to himself, he appeals to those who differ to consider the welfare of the teaching and the good of the community. Shinran had experienced persecution and the opposition of traditional Buddhist temples. He continued to experience government opposition against the spread of Pure Land teaching. He well knew that questionable behavior on the part of his followers would bring them into the eye of the government, with resulting restriction on their lives. Given an understanding of the authoritarian rigidity of the social and political structure that was the environment of those times in Japan, the appearance of disagreement and conflict in the community of Shinran's followers reflects a more democratic as well as more vital religious involvement as the disciples struggled to clarify the basis of their faith.

From another standpoint, we can see that disagreement is inevitable, since even people who are deeply motivated and hear the teaching from the same source can, because of differences in age, knowledge, and personality, differ on what they hear. Disagreement and misunderstanding must be treated with compassion now, too, as we become aware that we all have our differences.

Differences should be viewed as complementary rather than conflicting. By sharing differences and acknowledging them, we may mutually expand our horizons and deepen our insights. Yuien-bo furnishes an example, as does Shinran himself, of a person who could carefully maintain his own consistency of insight, while yet treating considerately and carefully the issues afflicting the community.

CHAPTER **17**

The Issue of Vow and Name

In chapter eleven, which is the first chapter in the second section of the *Tannisho*, Yuien-bo deals with issues which appear in many religions when people confuse correct doctrine with the reality of faith.

Sometimes followers use their knowledge as a means of demonstrating their superiority over others. Sometimes they attempt to use it to prove the depth of their faith. Often they have a "holier than thou" attitude.

Egoism in religion frequently clothes itself in robes of wisdom and piety. Yuien-bo, following the spirit of Shinran, warns of the futility of such attitudes and the harm done by them to other members as well as to the teaching itself.

The context and character of the issue Yuien-bo addresses in this chapter is the incidence of some members of the community approaching others and demanding to know if they understand properly the basis on which they recite the Nembutsu—was it on the basis of the mystery of the Vow or the mystery of the Name? These challengers might have argued that it is necessary to understand the true meaning of Nembutsu recitation in order to keep Shinran's teaching pure, and of course purity of faith is an important concern.

However, Shinran and Yuien-bo had a deeper concern— that of respect for personality and for the dignity of the individual. They never condemned with harsh language or attempted to embarrass those who opposed them. So, in this chapter, Yuien-bo laments that those who press this issue of the basis of the Nembutsu are intimidating people who are not learned and skilled in the texts. Not only do those who press this issue confuse others with their questions, but they indicate in the way they raise their questions that they themselves have not clarified the issues.

Thus Yuien-bo states that Amida, through his Vow, promised to save those who recite his Name, since the Name was easy to maintain. We are, accordingly, born into the Pure Land of True Recompense through the Original Vow. This birth in the Pure Land becomes assured in the very moment that we first believe in the Vow, and at the same time believe that our recitation is also due to the will of Amida and not at all a matter of our own self-will or calculation. Therefore, when we believe in the mystery of the Vow as our basic principle, the mystery of the Name is a natural consequence. Both aspects are in full harmony with no difference at all between them.

In contrast, however, if we intrude our own calculations and will into the situation and we believe that our rebirth depends on the good or evil deeds we do, then we are not relying on the mystery of the Vow. Rather, the Nembutsu we say in this case represents the striving of our minds for deeds that will purify us to produce our rebirth. This is self-effort, self-power.

Such people who do not understand the mystery of the Name truly, nevertheless finally attain the highest birth— though they may undergo a process of maturing, represented in the Pure Land mythology as being born in the land bordering the Pure Land, or in the land of sloth and pride, the castle of doubt, or the womb palace.

These symbols probably reflect early sectarian bias in the development of Pure Land teaching. They are used to encourage or stimulate reflection on one's spiritual condition.

The important point of chapter eleven is Yuien-bo's foresight that despite the possibility of error in one's conception of the process of faith, it is not the right of other people to try to intimidate followers—even presumably in the interests of true faith. Rather, there should be recognition of the breadth of Amida's compassion that finally embraces all.

As the time of each person's maturing arrives, one will come to understand the depth of faith and arrive at the highest realization.

On another level, the attitudes of those who question the nature of the other person's faith represents in itself a self-power and calculating way of dealing with the basic mystery of Pure Land faith and the mystery of life itself. Ultimately, everything will be embraced by Amida's compassion, just as purity and impurity become one in the vast sea.

The central issue of chapter eleven concerns the unity and harmony between the mystery of Amida's Vow and the mystery of his Name. The chapter correlates with Shinran's statement in chapter one that in the very moment we experience faith we are saved through the mystery of the Vow and the impulse to say Nembutsu arises. That same moment is the very moment of salvation when we are fully embraced by Amida's compassion. In other words, the mystery of the Name roots in the mystery of the Vow itself. It is through the Vow that the Name of Amida became validated as the way for common mortals to attain rebirth in the Pure Land.

The issue was not new to Yuien-bo. Among Shinran's letters, namely *Mattosho* #9, the same issue was taken up by Shinran. He responded to the question of Kyomyo-bo:

> I have read your letter very carefully.
>
> I fail to understand why your question should arise, for although we speak of Vow and of Name, these are not two different things. There is no Name separate from the Vow; there is no Vow separate from the Name. Even to say this, however, is to impose one's own calculation. Once you simply realize that the Vow surpasses conceptual understanding and with singleness of heart realize that the Name surpasses conceptual understanding and pronounce it, why should you labor in your own calculation?[1]

For Shinran, recitation of the Name followed upon faith in the Vow or—better—they were simultaneous. However, the true object of faith for Shinran was the Vow and its fulfillment as recorded in the *Larger Pure Land Sutra*. In earlier Pure Land tradition, emphasis lay on the Name itself as the practice designated by Amida's Vow and endowed with sacred power or purifying efficacy as indicated in the *Meditation Sutra*. Until the time of Shinran, faith generally centered on the validity of the practice of recitation. Shinran went beyond that to the source of the practice itself—in the Vow for the guarantee of salvation.

In every religion of salvation it is one thing to believe that one is saved or can be saved and another to have a deep inner assurance that one is actually saved. In the tradition of Nembutsu recitation, before and including Honen, there was the tendency to believe that the more one recited, the more sure one would become of eventual birth into the Pure Land. A quotation attributed to Honen states:

> If a man thinks that his attainment of birth is firmly settled, then it is settled; if he thinks it not, then it is not.[2]

This suggests a virtually self-induced faith and led to emphasis on the quantitive, repeated recitation of Nembutsu to increase one's certainty. This position invited intellectual and religious criticism by the opponents, as well as adherents, of Pure Land teaching. Thus Shinran declared in the volume on *Faith* of the *Kyogyoshinsho*:

> True faith is necessarily accompanied by (the utter-ance) of the Name. (The utterance of) the Name is not always accompanied by the Faith endowed by the Vow-power.[3]

For Shinran the assurance of salvation is given in the moment of spontaneity when, as a consequence of an encounter with the Vow, there is the impulse to recite the Nembutsu in grati-tude for the compassion perceived in the Vow.

Chapter eleven thus introduces us to a basic Dharmalogical problem arising from the elements of traditional Pure Land teaching. The problem signifies the shift from Honen's stress on the recitation of the Nembutsu as a means of salvation to Shinran's emphasis on the initial impulse of faith which stimulates the recitation. Yuien-bo's account of the issue of the basis for Nembutsu, as presented in this chapter, mirrors the struggle over what was primary and central to Pure Land teaching and what would provide the deepest assurance of rebirth.

Knowledge and Faith

In chapter twelve, Yuien-bo deals with issues very similar to those he discusses in chapter eleven, though in more detail. These issues revolve around the function of knowledge and study in religion, and the basis for salvation. Thus in chapter eleven, believers were challenged to defend their understanding of salvation through the distinction between the mystery of the Vow and the mystery of the Name. This was mainly an internal problem in the interests of purity of faith within the early Shinshu community.

Chapter twelve deals with the problem that arises when people are challenged to defend their faith by demonstrating knowledge of sutras and commentaries, a challenge based on the assumption that the more one knows, the more assured is salvation. This issue, while perhaps internal to Shinshu, appears also to involve people from other Buddhist traditions who questioned the authenticity of Shinshu teaching.

Before addressing the points made by Yuien-bo, I should like to place these discussions in the broader context of the history of religion. Though such arguments and challenges are unpleasant at times and even disruptive in a religious community, we should understand that they reflect a stage in the development of religion and actually indicate a deepening of religious awareness. Even sectarianism, as inconvenient and perhaps unnecessary as it appears, can be viewed as evidence of vitality in religion as people seek in a variety of ways to express truth or to renew spiritual experience.

The appearance of religious debate and sectarianism in history means that religion has transformed from communal folk conformity to personal decision and commitment. Religion is no longer merely an instrument to implement group goals and values. Rather, it has become a matter of personal insight and choice. There is a distinctive difference between natural, folk, or communal religion that relies on group compulsion, and individual religious faith which is voluntary and personal.

Faith and its basis only becomes an issue, and only remains vital, where there is a choice to be made. It is for this reason that in countries where there is a state religion, religious life is usually at a low ebb.

In the course of Buddhist history in Japan, Buddhism accommodated itself to the folk patterns of the Japanese based on tribal, clan, or regional requirements. The ancestral emphasis of Japanese Buddhism is the clearest evidence of this adaptation. At one point an emperor of Japan decreed that a *butsudan* (a Buddhist altar) be placed in every home— although he probably meant at least in every aristocratic home at that time. Provincial temples sponsored by the state for state welfare were established throughout the nation and staffed with official monks and nuns. In the earliest days in Japan, monks and nuns were conscripted for service in the temples.

In that earliest period, while many of the great teachers such as Saicho and Kukai entered the monastery out of personal choice, Buddhism was in the process of becoming a folk religion based on ancestral affiliation.

It was in the Kamakura period (1185–1332) that the Buddhist search for enlightenment and emancipation on a personal level flowered forth with a burst of creative movements, pioneered by Honen, then Shinran, Dogen, Ippen, and Nichiren. With the formation of personal faith, some intellectual understanding was necessary in order to make clear the break from traditional patterns of religion. When we survey the writings of these teachers, we find that they wrote in the language of the people, and their followers probed and questioned their faith.

In western terms, we would say that it was necessary to relate faith and reason. Faith required insight and knowledge in order to communicate to others. Reason needs faith to illumine the goal and attain assurance.

While all the teachers of this period would maintain that enlightenment is not a matter of intellectual exercise, their own scholarship indicates that they did not believe faith was a justification for ignorance, or that ignorance in itself was a virtue. When they referred to themselves as unknowing, ignorant, or stupid persons (as *Guchi no Honen-bo*), it did not mean that they thought they were actually that ignorant or that they revealed it. Rather, it meant they knew their limits and they did not use their knowledge as a weapon to show their superiority.

From the beginning, all the great Buddhist teachers attempted to inform and instruct their followers about the foundations of their faith among the varieties of human experience and belief. They never claimed that knowledge would create faith. They recognized that knowledge may sometimes be used to substitute or pose for faith.

To the great teachers, faith was simple and elemental to human existence, though knowledge and understanding may be complex. To confuse the issues and obscure the relation of faith and knowledge results in placing obstructions in the path of spiritual growth, in emptying religion of its liberating meaning. It also makes religion the monopoly of an elite, as Yuien-bo saw when he identified the demand for knowledge with the sage path tradition of Buddhism.

When we understand the background of the changes that took place in Buddhism during the Kamakura period, we can gain a glimpse of what is involved in order to make religion meaningful and vital in our own time of turmoil. It means to arouse commitment and to provide adequate insight to strengthen and articulate that commitment. Questioning and probing should be encouraged, and spiritual horizons broadened. Religious education becomes a primary need at all levels of personal development.

In this light, Yuien-bo's discussion in chapter twelve of the *Tannisho* takes on added significance as a sign of the deep spiritual awareness within the Shinshu community as well as the world at large as views clashed and people sought understanding.

Though Yuien-bo lamented the differences he observed, had they not occurred we should not have a glimpse of Shinran's teaching in such a creative form nor the glimpse of Yuien-bo's sensitive spirit. Despite the troublesome character of the disagreements lamented in the second section of the *Tannisho*, we see that these disagreements meant people had enough faith to raise the question and to think about it.

These issues remain in our own age. Many people— believers and unbelievers in religion—all tend to assume that religious faith cancels or makes unnecessary any intellectual reflection or inquiry or study. However, neither Shinran nor other Buddhist teachers ever advocated blind faith. They knew that if faith reflected the realities of human experience, it would never suffer from mere intellectual insight. They also knew that knowledge, like virtue or piety, could mask egoism and pride. Consequently, they urged their followers to consider carefully the relation of faith and knowledge.

It is against this background that Yuien-bo takes up the task of grappling with the place of knowledge in Shinshu faith.

CHAPTER **19**

Wisdom as Compassion

In chapter twelve of the *Tannisho*, the issue of the relationship of learning and salvation, or—perhaps—the problem of faith and reason in religion, is an issue that concerns all religions offering salvation. It marks a stage in the development of religion in history and, therefore, is a very important problem, requiring careful consideration. Distortion or overemphasis on either side will produce misunderstanding and conflict.

To stress the requirement of learning may make religion merely an intellectual exercise. To emphasize faith to the extreme may make a virtue of ignorance. What is required is a balance and an understanding of the role and function of each aspect of faith and learning.

When we study Shinran's writings, we observe that he does not object to learning in itself. His disciples and followers were knowledgeable in matters of Buddhism, as he was himself. However, he constantly indicated that faith or the salvation provided by Amida's Vow was difficult to understand or conceive. He warned against the pride that comes when we believe we can grasp everything by intellectual reflection. He was deeply aware, as was Honen before him, of the depth of the mystery that surrounds human existence. He understood well that our minds are limited in ability and influenced by passion and egoism. It is only when we understand these conditions that our reason and our faith can work in harmony.

With this background, Yuien-bo attacks the demand made by some members of the early Shinshu community that people who do not read or study sutras cannot be certain of their birth into the Pure Land. Yuien-bo replies that this view is clearly in error, since the sutras make it clear that birth is due to faith in the Original Vow and the practice of Nembutsu. No quantity of learning is made a requirement. Rather, if one is not aware of the way of rebirth presented by the Vow, one should study it more closely.

Study is not necessary for salvation, but it may be necessary to clarify the intention of the Vow. Honen, in his *Senjaku-shu*, the manifesto of Pure Land teaching, had clearly indicated that if Amida had made the object of his Vow to save those who were learned and well-versed in affairs, few would have been saved, because the learned and wise are few and the ignorant are many.

Religious paths which require certain learning or special knowledge create elites and special classes. Some people are superior and others, inferior. This, according to Honen and Shinran, is totally against the purpose of the Original Vow. It is significant that spiritual equality is a feature of Pure Land faith that made it appealing to the masses.

Yuien-bo goes on to point out that the way of the Nembutsu is what is traditionally called the "Easy Path" in contrast to the difficult ways of the "Sage" or "Holy Path." Many people have misunderstood the significance of the so-called "Easy" way as something for lazy people. However, such is not the case. It is easy because Amida has made the way which would be most available for all types of people. It is easy because its basis and fulfillment depend on Amida.

What is difficult about it is the challenge it presents to the ego to give up its pretensions and its pride; its demand that we look more deeply within ourselves and admit our boundedness and our evils. Shinran recognized that it is most difficult for people to give up their calculating, competitive, selfish minds.

The Sage Path or Holy Path, which promotes wisdom and knowledge as the way to salvation, is easy because it fits the human predisposition to think in terms of success, reward and punishment, or self-justification, and to find something to demonstrate one's superiority over others. Without specifying particular teachings which Shinran and Yuien-bo had in mind as they taught their followers, we should consider the "Easy" way and the "Holy Path" as symbols for certain kinds of spiritual attitudes that appear among religious people in all traditions.

Shinran was very much aware that religion could mask egoism as well as expose it. Only that religion which exposes the insidious and subtle ways of ego even in religious people can provide salvation in this life, let alone in any future life.

There is a deeper issue lying behind the problem of knowledge and salvation. That deeper issue is: no amount of learning and knowledge can assure the truth of one's faith.

It is clear that argumentation never really converts anyone, nor does piling up verses and texts create faith. The root of faith is not in knowledge or information. We do not come to believe something or attain faith by merely acquiring information. Rather, faith grasps us; it is awakened within us. We can only acknowledge it.

Shinran viewed his understanding of faith by seeing it as a gift, a bestowal of Amida Buddha's true mind manifesting within our own minds. It is *monbo*—hearing, that is, receiving Dharma; rather than *shugyo*—cultivating Dharma.

In this view, faith involves the totality of a person's being. It is what he is and not merely what he believes. Belief and knowledge pertain to the intellectual faculties which can be diverse in people but which are stimulated through the deep resources of faith in the person.

Whatever the subtle issues which may be involved in the consideration of faith and intellect, it appears that both during and after Shinran's lifetime among his followers, debates took place in which the merits of one side or the other were argued. Yuien-bo deplored the tendency of people to claim that their teaching was superior and others inferior. He makes an important point that when arguments arouse passions such as hatred and anger, one really damages oneself. Slandering another's teaching ends really in slandering one's own. The bitterness that results from argument is self-degrading.

In our own contemporary competitive religious world, Shinran's insight is well worth considering. It should never be necessary to advance one's spiritual insight and recommend it to others by denouncing alternative views. Buddhism has always been a tolerant faith, not out of indifference, but out of basic respect for personality and an understanding of the relativity of views in relation to the depth and profundity of the truth and reality.

Yuien-bo advised the followers of Nembutsu to practice their faith quietly, recognizing that they were limited in their abilities and that the way of faith was designed for them. It is the intention of the Buddha to provide a way suitable for all. In this second section of the *Tannisho*, Yuien-bo calls attention to the fact that Buddha prophesied such adversity, and clearly implies in chapter twelve that abuse or opposition is an opportunity for faith to become deeper.

So, in face of the many problems that beset the followers of Nembutsu, Yuien-bo suggests that one should not study merely to be able to suppress or refute the views of others. Rather, study should be pursued to become more deeply aware of the meaning of the Vow and faith in Amida. It should be used to help people.

Knowledge should always be motivated by compassion. Hence, if a person doubted that one could ever be saved, one might help them understand Amida's compassion and give hope. It is a basic point in Buddhism that wisdom is never in contradiction to compassion. Wisdom always has its aim in realizing and manifesting the compassion that is the essence of Buddha.

In the final analysis, the requirement "to study" in Buddhism is not to qualify for salvation, but to manifest the quality of compassion.

CHAPTER **20**

The Issue of Morality

The *Tannisho*'s chapter thirteen provides an interesting glimpse into the depth of Shinran's teaching and the determination of Yuien-bo to apply it consistently and carefully.

As we have frequently noted, religion often masks a deep egoism. In chapter twelve of the *Tannisho*, Yuien-bo pointed out how people put on intellectual airs in order to exhibit their superiority. In chapter thirteen, the issue revolves around those who would use morality as a means of showing superiority.

In Pure Land teaching, the problem taken up in this chapter has a long background among Honen's disciples and also among those of Shinran. Mention of this problem appears frequently in Shinran's letters and caused him considerable pain and disappointment. The instigators of the problem were people who claimed that it was permissible to fulfill one's desires in any way, because the Original Vow promised to save all sinners no matter how evil.

This interpretation became known in Shinshu as *hongan-bokori*, conceit or pride in the Vow. It carried the logic and intent of Amida's Vow to save to extremes to justify one's egoistic behavior.

In chapter three of the *Tannisho*, Yuien-bo quoted Shinran's declaration that the object of the Original Vow was the evil person. Shinran himself understood that his declaration—if the good person can be saved, even more so would the evil person—was contrary to the usual way of human thinking. It was subtle thought and apparently easily misinterpreted to mean that evil deeds in no way could be a barrier to salvation.

Shinran, of course, opposed moralistic approaches to salvation that made goodness the source of salvation. For him, the compassion that brings salvation was totally the work of Amida Buddha, and not limited by human moral requirements or limitations. Amida had vowed to save all beings bound by delusion and passion.

Shinran's assertion of the primacy of the evil person was intended to dispel fear, guilt, and anxiety in those ordinary persons who could not perform the more rigorous Buddhist practices aimed at enlightenment. However, it is evident that some disciples used the principle to justify their careless and thoughtless behavior. They believed they would be saved in spite of their immoral or evil acts.

The error of extreme reliance or pride in the Vow lies in that manner of moral complacency and indifference by those who use the Vow as an excuse for egoism. The Vow, however, is intended to liberate us from the bondage of ego. As the sun melts ice into water, so the Vow desired to transform the ice of egoism into the water of compassion.

Shinran himself was not indifferent to moral issues. He was most concerned that his disciples should not distort or misinterpret the teaching and bring it into disrepute in the wider community. At times he appealed to them not to give the government authorities an excuse to persecute them. He also emphasized that it is foolish to take poison merely because there is an antidote.

When Yuien-bo encountered this issue after Shinran's death, some new factors had entered in. Perhaps in response to Shinran's appeals for proper behavior as an expression of gratitude for the Vow's compassion, some members took it upon themselves to enforce good order among the followers. They went so far as to hang up notices in the temples that persons committing sins should not enter.

Yuien-bo was, therefore, faced with a conflict of views among the followers on what was the correct view of the situation. There were those whose spiritual conceit led them to use the Vow for their own satisfactions, while others attempted to establish moral behavior as a criterion for faith in the Vow. There was self-righteousness on both sides, which Yuien-bo considered equally contradictory and in opposition to Shinran's teaching. Paradoxically, the Vow neither justified immoral behavior nor required moral behavior.

In order to grasp the problem of moral behavior in relation to salvation, Yuien-bo directs our attention to the teaching of karma set forth by Shinran. He provides an interesting conversation he had with the master in which Shinran asked Yuien-bo if he believed everything that Shinran told him. Yuien-bo, of course, agreed. He also affirmed that he would not disobey Shinran.

Then Shinran asked him, "Would you murder a thousand people if it would guarantee your birth in the Pure Land?"

Yuien-bo answered that he could not even kill a single person.

Shinran retorted, "Why, then, did you say you would obey me completely?"

On the basis of this interchange, Shinran goes on to explain that all our acts, whether good or bad, are the outcome of past karma. Therefore, we really have no good deeds to be proud of, or offer for salvation—nor are our evil deeds an obstruction to the Vow.

In the case of the dispute among the followers which is related in chapter thirteen, Yuien-bo, following Shinran's insight, maintained that those people who used the Vow to justify their misdeeds were assuredly saved because of their faith in the Vow, while their deeds were the working out of their karmic process. On the other hand, those who stress the requirement of morality are implying doubt in the Vow because they demand that a person root out passions and lusts in order truly to receive the benefit of the Vow. According to Yuien-bo, to press for moral behavior as a requirement makes the Vow useless.

Although Shinran places great emphasis on the role of karma in human behavior, he constantly advocated and pleaded with his followers to act with respect and propriety toward the members of their community, society, and other religious groups. He does not reject free will and the need for moral action as the basis of human relations. It is at this point that the issues of time and eternity, the absolute and the relative, fate and free will, intersect in Shinran's teaching.

The issue of salvation, free will, and morality appears in many religions, notably Christianity, Islam, and in some forms of Hinduism. It became a major issue in the West and has been difficult to resolve.

Shinran's way of salvation and the view of karma he sets forth are addressed to people who find themselves driven—seemingly against their will—into situations they cannot control. Shinran himself saw this in terms of social roles, such as farmer, hunter, fisherman, merchant, or perhaps warrior, into which people were born in ancient society and which they could little change. Shinran's conversation with Yuien-bo in chapter thirteen reflects the predicament of the warriors who must kill even though personally they do not desire to do so.

We all have needs and desires or drives which frequently dictate behavior and create personal problems. Shinran sought to assure such people that salvation was completely the result of the Vow and did not require an impossible feat of will or purification on their part.

Thus, for Shinran, taking the totality of existence into account, the compassion of Amida embraced the whole of the karmic process. In the first chapter of the first part of the *Tannisho*, Shinran stated that no evil could obstruct the Vow and no good was superior to it.

Shinran's faith is a faith beyond good and evil, because it is not subject to the human criteria of good and evil for its realization. Therefore, on the social level, no one can presume to judge when that salvation is realized in a person or not. This is also why he said he had not even one disciple. No one was to stand in judgment on another.

Nevertheless, even though human behavior is rooted in karma, Shinran believed that evil behavior which could be avoided should be—not for the sake of gaining or assuring salvation, but out of gratitude for Amida's compassion and for the good of the community.

Like other thinkers, Shinran appealed to people on the basis of their experience of freedom and ability to choose. Consistent with Buddhist teaching, he did not take the facts of conscious experience as totally representing the state of ultimate reality. Rather, he emphasized that it is the realm of delusion.

The reality of the Vow and its compassion illuminates and determines our experience. Our experience does not limit the Vow. Despite the conflict, the Vow embraces all, transcending all factions. In this lies its truth and grandeur.

The Embrace That Inspires

Chapter fourteen of the *Tannisho* involves an ongoing issue among the followers of Shinran concerning the meaning and function of the Nembutsu, the recitation of the Buddha's Name.

This chapter correlates with chapter eight of the first section, which presents the Nembutsu as a non-practice, a non-good. Yuien-bo quotes Shinran as explaining that the Nembutsu is not a practice because it is not done by our own intention and deliberation. It is a non-good, because its good does not derive from our own plan or calculation. He stresses that the Nembutsu is, rather, a manifestation of Amida's compassion implanted within us. It is a spontaneous and free act which wells up within us as we become aware of the compassion that embraces our lives.

Shinran's teaching in his letters and other writings is very clear on the meaning of the Nembutsu; but confusion could arise among his disciples because of the traditional understanding of the Nembutsu in Pure Land Buddhism and in popular Buddhism. In Buddhism generally, all practices (including the recitation of a Buddha's name) produced good karma or merit which would yield various benefits in this life or the next. This conception, based on the principles of karma and transmigration, goes back to earliest times in Indian religion, as well as in Buddhism.

The Pure Land teaching, based on the three Pure Land sutras, assumed these principles, although it made the recitation of Amida Buddha's Name the most effective way to gain such merit or to purify people from aeons and aeons of accumulated karmic pollution. The most important passage setting forth this way of hope and salvation appears in the Pure Land *Meditation Sutra.*

This text teaches that even the most sinful and evil person, who has committed the ten evil deeds and the five deadly sins and who has never before recited the Nembutsu, can be purified of eight billions of aeons of sins through the recitation of the Nembutsu on his deathbed. The more they recite, the more purification takes place.

In later centuries, until the time of Shinran, the hope and compassion that inspired this passage in the ancient sutra became the foundation for the popular development of Amidist Pure Land teaching.

Despite the influence and importance of this passage and its principle of salvation for the lowest degree of humanity, Yuien-bo, following the teaching of Shinran, declared that, so far as the text implies that we can purify our own evils through the practice of Nembutsu, this text does not reach the depth of teaching set forth by Shinran concerning the meaning of the Nembutsu.

According to Yuien-bo, Shinran taught that the Nembutsu only has the function of expressing our gratitude for Amida Buddha's compassion, which is the true source of salvation. The Nembutsu arises spontaneously from our awareness of faith and the assurance we receive within ourselves that our destiny is determined once and for all.

This idea is hinted at in chapter one of the *Tannisho,* when Shinran speaks of the moment when the thought to recite the Nembutsu arises. It is in that intuitive moment that salvation, or the embrace of Amida, is realized and manifested for us. At that moment, the Nembutsu is a freely inspired or spontaneous surge in the mind and heart. It expresses the joy and gratitude we feel when we receive the flash of insight that our salvation does not depend on the fitful, irregular, calculating, or egoistic efforts that we perform, but roots in an all-embracing reality that gives us life and supports us at every moment.

In chapter fourteen, Yuien-bo explores a problem raised by the sutra itself, a problem which indicates the uncertainty and anxiety accompanying the Nembutsu of purification. According to the sutra, the person of the lowest degree is deserving of the greatest retribution for many aeons. However, if—on his deathbed—he meets a good friend who tries to help him meditate and think on the Buddha, he can even then attain a good rebirth. However, if his illness is too severe and the pain is so intense that the individual is incapable of sustaining meditation on the Buddha, he may then recite the Name of Buddha ten times with sincerity and without interruption as a means to gain a good rebirth. Each recitation will purify him of aeons and aeons of sins.

As hopeful as this alternative is in the scale of beings set forth in the sutra, Yuien-bo points out that if it is necessary for us to purify our own sins, we are confronted with a serious problem. We would have to recite the Nembutsu at every moment in our lives, because we are constantly piling up evil karma through our egoistic thoughts and actions. Even more telling, for Yuien-bo, is the fact that our karma condition may result in sudden and untimely death or such agonizing suffering that would make it impossible to keep the purifying Nembutsu in our minds. Thus it would be virtually impossible to be assured of rebirth.

We might add here an additional consideration in line with Yuien-bo's thought. As our sins which bind us to the wheel of birth and death are essentially infinite, as we emerge from the infinite, unknown past in our endless repetition of life and death, we cannot know the depth and extent of our depravity that has kept us chained to the wheel of rebirths. It thus becomes ambiguous and uncertain how a specific number of recitations could erase such a weighty and incalculable bondage.

It is a paradoxical religious question how a finite, human act can resolve an infinite, spiritual problem. When has the person done enough? Who can know this? If one looks at it on the practical level, we can see why, in Buddhist history, the great saints are recorded as reciting the Nembutsu as much as sixty thousand times a day. It required prodigious effort and concentration to acquire the spiritual potential to wipe out the load of depravity we drag through our karmic destinies.

This belief also provided the basis for the wide range of Buddhist ceremonies designed to enlist the help of relatives in securing a destiny for the departed which, with their limited efforts, they may not have been able to do for themselves. Although these beliefs reflect aspects of Buddhist compassion, they also gave rise to anxiety concerning the destiny of the departed.

It is at this point that Shinran's teaching reveals its importance in the development of Buddhist doctrine. Shinran endeavored to meet this anxiety by perceiving in the Pure Land teaching the true basis of salvation. He saw that the initiative and basis for salvation lay in actuality in the divine reality and not in the mere human act. The divine reality embraces and manifests itself through the human act. It inspires the human act. Further, he pressed beyond the physical or vocal limitations of the act and focused on the deeper level of human awareness which stimulates the act.

In essence, for Shinran, salvation lies not in the *act*, but in the conviction and deep faith which arises spontaneously and intuitively within us when we encounter the teaching of Amida. Thus he speaks of the *shin* (or *shinjin*) *no ichinen*, the one moment, the one thought, when faith is realized. This is also why Shinran equates *monbo*—hearing the Dharma— with faith.

In that deep moment, the moment of insight, our destiny becomes finally determined and our response becomes one of gratitude and joy. It is, perhaps, difficult for us to imagine the relief and emancipation experienced by Shinran and his followers when they experienced this transforming moment.

As the Shinshu community developed, it had great implications for the nature of religious life.

This reinterpretation of the meaning of religious practice in Shinshu led to the rejection of all traditional Buddhist disciplines used to purify the mind or body. Monasticism was no longer required. Hence Shinran married and raised a family. He also ate meat. Shinran's teaching allowed people to develop their lives in a positive manner. Repressive moralistic behavior, long employed to define the required "good deeds" gained a more positive role as the expression of gratitude for Buddha's compassion.

Later, Rennyo Shonin revitalized the Shinshu community by showing how reliance on Amida Buddha abolished anxiety and superstition. The *myokonin*, lay saints, express the joy and the spiritual freedom that results from confident faith. For Shinran and his followers, the meaning of life is not in struggling against an uncertain destiny, but in living with gratitude for the compassion that sustains our being.

CHAPTER **22**

An Understanding of Limitations

In contrast to some schools of Buddhism, which maintain that we may attain Buddhahood and—implicit in such attainment—perfection in this life, Shinshu emphasizes that we are ever and always passion-ridden common mortals, saved in spite of our imperfections.

Chapter fifteen of the *Tannisho* addresses the claims to human perfection that are advanced by some traditions in Buddhism. In this chapter we have a clear view of the contrast between Shinshu and other Buddhist teachings concerning the spiritual status of the believer in this life.

The issue arises out of the development of Buddhist tradition which has always assumed the possibility of human perfectibility through performance of the prescribed disciplines of Buddhism. Although Buddhism held this ideal, it also maintained that it would take numerous lives or rebirths in order to fully achieve it and gain Nirvana. One could never assert that one had attained perfection in this life, however. To claim that one had achieved the status of an Arhat, the worthy one who has done all that there is to be done, was a serious spiritual offense.

When Buddhism took root in China, the goal of Buddhist discipline was reinterpreted under the influence of the doctrine that all beings possess Buddha-nature. Buddhist discipline now aimed at the realization of one's Buddha-nature in this very existence as a sudden, transforming awareness of one's unity with all things.

The ideal was developed most notably in Zen Buddhism, with its unique methods to cultivate the awareness and to test it. It also took shape in the Shingon tradition. Here it was believed that the practice of mudras, intricate hand and finger symbolism, recitation of potent phrases and chants called mantras, as well as profound meditations, would result in a deep experience of vision and union with Mahavairocana Buddha, the essence of the cosmos. This ideal was summarized in the phrase *Sokushin-jobutsu*, "becoming a Buddha in this very body."

In Tendai, using similar practices together with the detailed system of meditations worked out by the great Tendai master in China, Chigi (538–97), the goal was to experience *ichinen sanzen*, the three thousand things in one thought or moment— the experience of the total unity of all things within oneself in a flash of insight and awareness. While it remains a question as to what extent the achievement of these forms of consciousness also meant the attainment of actual perfection in the individual, it is clear that they had great influence in Japan when they were introduced by Kukai and Saicho in the ninth century. They were also very vigorous and demanding disciplines as preparation for enlightenment.

The foundation of such teachings in Buddhism was the doctrine of non-duality. This ideal or principle dissolved the barriers between the past, present, and future. It is a general feature of Mahayana Buddhism to stress the centrality of the present life and its experience as the focal point for the attainment of enlightenment. Even in our own time this note has had great influence and appeal. "Now" is the only context where we can attain spiritual goals.

Shinran and Yuien-bo modified the perspective of traditional Mahayana Buddhism concerning the relation of the present and future in the process of attaining enlightenment. Their point of view, stressed in the *Tannisho*'s chapter fifteen, maintained the realism of the Pure Land interpretation of human nature and its limitations as inevitably passion-ridden and egoistic, a theme that is indeed central to both parts of the *Tannisho.*

From the Shinshu perspective, we gain the assurance of our future enlightenment in the Pure Land in this life. Nevertheless, the final realization lies in the future. Thus Shinran and Yuien-bo attempted through the experience of faith to exalt the importance of this life, the "Now," in line with Mahayana Buddhism. At the same time, they avoided the arrogance of claims to enlightenment on the part of mere common mortals. They recognized that as long as we are in our present finite and worldly bodies, we are constantly afflicted by our passions and the distortions of egoism.

To dramatize the paradox of such claims, Yuien-bo calls attention in chapter fifteen to the nature of Buddha as depicted in tradition. To become a Buddha essentially meant to achieve perfection in every way. To show the impossibility of this for common mortals, Yuien-bo calls attention to the fact that at the end of their lives, even devotees of the other paths pray for their eventual enlightenment in another life. According to Yuien-bo, this prayer or aspiration is a recognition of the immense difficulty of transcending or abolishing the ego and passions.

Further, Buddhist tradition details that a true Buddha possesses the thirty-two major marks of a great man, as well as eighty secondary features. These characteristics symbolize the total spiritual and physical perfection in a Buddha. According to Yuien-bo, no one who has practiced the disciplines can claim to have these signs of perfection. In general, he is correct in his assessment. However, if he meant to take the symbols literally, it is probable that there was no such real expectation in the teachings of those traditions.

In the Mahayana understanding of Buddhahood, the ideal was to attain a sense of oneness with the whole, or emptiness—as in Tendai—the truth of the Middle, where things are Void, yet are as they are. The issue here between Shinshu and other traditions is to experience one's Buddha-nature as against becoming a specific Buddha.

Allowing for whatever polemical or sectarian perspective Yuien-bo expresses, his point is still sound that it is arrogant to strive for, or claim, perfection in this life as we experience it. Further, we should observe that such efforts are elitist, and could only be performed and attained—if at all—by the best of people.

As Shinran was aware in his own life, practices conceived as one's own effort toward a goal are competitive and create self-righteousness. Even the most sublime practices become detriments to spirituality and to Buddhism if they merely become ways to discriminate one person from the other.

It is the distinction of Pure Land teaching to offer salvation to all, good or evil. A person attains certainty of salvation in the Pure Land in the moment of faith regardless of his or her actual sinful character or what practice he or she might be engaged in.

The intent of the *Tannisho's* fifteenth chapter is to urge the followers of Shinran not to confuse the meaning of Shinshu by paralleling or interpreting it in terms of other teachings then current or popular. The assurance of Amida's embrace is not the same as the attainment of Buddhahood in this life. The fact that we are emancipated from the stream of birth and death through faith is not the same as enlightenment.

Such confusion of principles undermines the universality and realism of Shinran's teachings, as well as produces the arrogance and pride reflected in other points of controversy with which Yuien-bo has been dealing in earlier chapters. This issue remains of vital concern today.

In our contemporary situation we may see in Yuien-bo's analysis a comment on the general idea that all religions are the same. This idea, now so commonly expressed, produces indifference and confusion in religious thinking as well as helps to create many of our social problems. What is needed in dealing with contemporary issues is clear thinking, such as Yuien-bo exhibits. We need a sound understanding of the various spiritual principles that inspire and motivate the diverse teachings in religion. An understanding of the differences, as well as similarities, among the religions, is essential in establishing strong personal convictions and developing meaningful interfaith relations.

Above all, Yuien-bo is emphasizing that the real essence of religion is humility, an understanding of limitations.

No amount of claims to exalted spiritual status or power can establish the reality and truth of faith. Such claims may only be the sign of an exalted ego.

The compassion which is the ultimate expression of religious reality can only be glimpsed in and through a life of humility.

CHAPTER **23**

Religion as Positive Experience

There is an interesting relationship between chapter sixteen and the preceding chapter in which the issue of perfection was taken up.

In chapter fifteen, Yuien-bo made it clear that in all that it really means in this lifetime, no one could claim to attain Buddhahood. We remain passion-ridden mortals in this life, but in our future life we are assured of rebirth and final enlightenment.

In chapter sixteen, the realistic situation in which believers get angry or do evil things such as getting into disputes with fellow believers is addressed. No matter what people believe, they do not always express the ideal all the time in their lives. However, those in the community who tended to be moralistically inclined maintained that fellow believers whose behavior was not exemplary must repent and transform their minds.

Yuien-bo, relating this, quickly drew the distinction that the call for constant repentance suggested by these moralistic people reflected the traditional Buddhist principle of ceasing to do evil and practicing good, rather than the basic principle of Shinran's teaching. The moralists' position was that the evildoers were to purify themselves and acquire merit. To remind them of the very different essence of Shinran's teaching, Yuien-bo pointed out once again that the followers of the single-hearted, sole practice of Nembutsu experience have this so-called transformation of mind and heart only one time in a conversion which results from the penetration of the power of the Original Vow into the depths of the person, a penetration that works a transformation in one's awareness of Amida Buddha's compassion.

This transformation based on the Original Vow offers complete assurance of rebirth, while the relative and repeated transformation demanded by those who try to purify from evils is directed only to specific misdeeds. It provides no final assurance.

According to Yuien-bo, the fundamental transformation based on Amida's Vow takes place when a person who has not known the true teaching of the Nembutsu by Other Power based on the Original Vow comes to rely on the Original Vow, and, under the influence of Amida's wisdom, deeply realizes his basic inability to achieve enlightenment through his own efforts.

When this transformation occurs, there is a reorientation in the self in which the habitual, customary ways of thinking about religion fall aside as the recognition of the embrace of Amida Buddha (the embrace which does not reject) grows. This recognition reflects the teaching of the two types of deep faith in which the radiation of Amida's compassion arouses awareness of both our evil self and the embrace of Amida's compassion for that self.

In essence, this awareness means a profound self-acceptance which accepts oneself as one is. We become thus released from the fears and anxieties and frustrations of our personal evils, knowing that ultimately reality, as expressed in the symbol of Amida Buddha, accepts us as we are.

The constant frustration and guilt that derives from our efforts to purify ourselves are frequently projected outward onto other people, and become the source of much personal conflict. There is a profound psychological significance—as well as philosophical insight—in Shinran's teaching. The attempts at self-purification may encourage efforts at self-justification and make it impossible for people to recognize or admit their evils.

Astutely, Yuien-bo points out that if we must repent day and night for our evils, we can never be assured of final salvation, since we may die in an instant. Life does not wait for us to inhale or exhale. We may reach the end of our lives without ever living with mild and forbearing thoughts or without ever achieving this transformation of mind and heart. In effect, the constant struggle for purity of the self renders Amida Buddha's Original Vow meaningless.

He points out, however, that there are those who talk about salvation through the Other Power of the Original Vow, but yet at the same time harbor in their hearts a doubt concerning the Vow even when, intellectually, they believe the Vow saves evil people. People with uncertain faith will be reborn in the neighboring region of the Pure Land as depicted in the mythology set forth in the sutra.

However, if faith is determined, rebirth is totally the work of Amida Buddha and not the result of human calculations or deliberations. Hence, even if we do evil things, a mind of mildness and forbearance will gradually grow as more and more we revere the power of the Original Vow. This mildness and forbearance naturally springs forth when we constantly reflect on the depth of the Buddha's compassion toward us. It is with this awareness that we recite the Nembutsu.

This is the basis of the principle of Naturalness and Spontaneity in Shinran's teaching. The Nembutsu is spontaneous because it wells up from deep in the human spirit and is not based on some intention or calculation of benefit to be gained from it.

In chapter sixteen, the major issue in Yuien-bo's considerations is: What provides the focus of religious life? Is religion merely a negative aspect of life and directed only at avoiding evil deeds or repenting of our failures? Or is religion a positive force in which, despite the lapses and failures we experience in living up to our ideals, our hearts become attuned to the compassion we find flowing through life?

The principle set forth in chapter sixteen suggests that religion is a positive experience, through which we become naturally and spontaneously transformed into the ideal toward which our mind is turned. That is, to the extent that the Nembutsu and the symbol of Amida Buddha, the manifestation of infinite compassion, penetrates imperceptibly but deeply into our lives, we develop minds that are compassionate and embracing. There is thus an assimilation of the ideal to which the mind is directed as Amida embraces us.

The discussion in chapter sixteen indicates that Yuien-bo and Shinran were not without ethical and moral concerns. However, they did not advocate a repressive approach to ethical life. It was, for them, not a question of doing good or trying to be good, but of becoming good as the compassion of Amida penetrated one's spirit.

In society and much of moral life, the repressive way of morality appears to be the most efficient and strongest way to gain good behavior. Rules, regulations, and laws all attempt to repress certain forms of behavior through threat of punishment and retaliation. Parents frequently use such methods in dealing with their children and the pattern is absorbed into children at an early age. Hence, they try to be good in order to win approval and avoid punishment. Sometimes the pattern is deep enough to create severe guilt and mental problems.

There are limits to the effectiveness of repressive morality, because everything is made to depend on whether one gets caught or not. It also provokes rebellion and hypocrisy, both being sources of great problems in society and personal life. The fear and threats involved in such an approach to behavior often produces the very opposite of what is desired by the repressive community.

Yuien-bo suggests a way of displacement and replacement. We need not try to root out the evil which has been imbedded so deeply in our nature. Rather, through associating and identifying with positive ideals of compassion, when we come to see that this is what gives meaning to life, we move gradually over time and with mutual support from others engaged in a similar process, toward the transformation of mind and spirit that are the basis of sound behavior.

In effect, we have in chapter sixteen an "Other Power" approach to the problem of ethics which does not compromise the teaching in order to ensure that believers will be socially acceptable. It is important to note that since the person undergoing this process is deeply aware of his or her own evil, the transformation which takes place does not encourage or promote self-righteousness such as occurs when people try to be good.

Instead, the spontaneous expressions of gratitude which stimulate proper and good human relations are all seen as resulting from Amida's compassion that now inspires our lives. Thus all forms of spiritual and ethical competitiveness are ruled out. Religious faith becomes a completely inward, spontaneous reality.

There is here also an emphasis on growth. As the awareness of compassion grows deeper, the quality of our lives, our aspirations and ideals, becomes deeper.

The principle of Naturalness and Spontaneity that underlay Shinran's teaching means simply that religion is life, and life is religion.

Faith transforms life, and our living becomes the expression of our faith.

The Issue of Hell

While the *Tannisho*'s chapter sixteen concerned problems of purification and repentance in this life, chapter seventeen relates to issues of the afterlife.

In both chapters, Yuien-bo confronts the problems directly and preserves the spirit of Shinran's teaching of absolute compassion as the basis of enlightenment and emancipation. Just as in chapter sixteen he showed that Shinran's teaching did not require constant effort in repentance or conversion, nor advocate an ethic of repression, so in this chapter he indicates that Shinran's teaching does not rely on or create a sense of fear for one's future life as a means to stimulate religious belief or commitment.

In the background of chapter seventeen there was a situation in which certain members held that people who lacked a true understanding and faith in Amida's Original Vow would be born into a borderland of the Pure Land after their death. From there, they would fall into hell.

Even on the face of it, this notion hardly sounds compassionate toward those who have difficulty in grasping the depth of Shinran's teaching of the Original Vow. In no uncertain terms, Yuien-bo rejects this idea as being without foundation in the sutras and commentaries. He raises questions about the way such people study the texts. Whatever they intend, they imply in their interpretation that Amida's compassion is vain and that the Buddha has deceived us concerning the way to enlightenment.

If we consider for a moment what the party whom Yuien-bo opposes might have been aiming at, we might be able to clarify the issue behind this short chapter. It is stated that the number of devotees with true faith were few. Shinran himself has indicated frequently that true faith is difficult to attain, though birth in the Pure Land is easy.

There is a paradox of human experience here, in which the proclamation of Amida's compassion is too good to be true. People dominated by the ordinary religious mode typified as self-power have great difficulty in believing in absolute compassion. Thus, they remain indifferent—or even oppose the teaching of Amida's absolute compassion.

It is possible that those who asserted that such people who had doubts might fall into hell were actually attempting to stimulate their own self-reflection as to where their doubt of Amida might ultimately lead them. However, Yuien-bo points out that such an assertion, rather than clarifying the meaning of Amida's compassion, actually contradicts it and renders it a lie.

If it were possible for anyone ultimately to go to hell, Amida's Vow would be meaningless, since he vowed that he would not accept enlightenment unless all other beings were enlightened with him. Ultimately, with Amida's Vow fulfilled, there could not remain an unenlightened person.

The indivisible and inclusive nature of the Vow requires a faith that, ultimately, all are now and ultimately will be saved. Shinran points out it is ten kalpas since the Vow was completed. Hence, emancipation is now real, as his teaching shows.

For Yuien-bo it was not at all necessary to threaten people with the possibility of falling into hell in order to awaken their religious insight and faith in the Vow. The symbols of the afterlife in Pure Land teaching have a deeper positive significance in helping us to understand that while religious awakening comes to individuals at different times in their life experience, even those who depart this life without such definite experience will ultimately attain it in whatever state they find themselves in that future world.

The absolute compassion of Amida, that embraces and does not reject—which we may experience in this life—also includes the next life. From the absolute standpoint, all are really saved. However, from the standpoint of relative human experience, we must all pass through a process leading to the moment of faith.

The symbols of various regions and conditions preceding birth into the Pure Land, symbols such as the borderland, the castle of doubt, or the womb palace, all express the sense of nearness to final enlightenment, or the potentiality of everyone to attain it. It is significant that Shinran preserves the positive symbolism of Pure Land teaching as the means of giving hope to the people of his time, but nowhere in his teaching does he threaten or teach that people fall into hell as a consequence of their failure to perceive the depth of Amida's compassion.

This issue, as presented by Yuien-bo, indicates how acutely Shinran perceived the depth of the Mahayana Buddhist idea of compassion. Mahayana Buddhism emphasizes the centrality of compassion as a quality indispensable for the attainment of wisdom. There can be no wisdom apart from compassion. The figure of the Bodhisattva reveals the character of this religion and the essential meaning of life.

When viewed from this standpoint, all forms of symbolism in Mahayana Buddhism are to be seen as aids to stimulate the spiritual growth of the person toward enlightenment. It is not to be used merely to inspire fear and anxiety. Thus, the Buddhist mythology of afterlife and destiny is a matter of hope, even when there are negative symbols suggesting punishment and suffering in the afterlife.

On the one hand, Buddhism is a realistic philosophy in recognizing the infinite varieties of people and beings. There is a hierarchy of beings based on spiritual development, as is stated in the Pure Land *Meditation Sutra*. On the other hand, Buddhism is not morally indifferent. It recognizes the continuum of human action from good to evil in various degrees.

The teaching of Dharma associated with this system emphasizes that our destinies are brought upon ourselves. There is a sense of judgment in Buddhism, but it is not arbitrary nor does it remove the responsibility from the person.

Buddhism is rigorous in emphasizing personal responsibility. It is the paradox of religious teaching that the aspect which highlights personal responsibility may, in view of the essential weakness of human beings, cultivate a sense of despair and anxiety at the impossibility of ever attaining the highest spiritual ideals. Religious institutions have used this anxiety as a means to secure support by relieving those anxieties through rituals and consoling teachings.

The remarkable feature of Shinran's teaching is that he did not employ these beliefs as a means merely to gain followers. Rather, he constantly pointed to the compassion of Amida in such a way that he even limited control over his own followers (as indicated in chapter six of the *Tannisho*), and was led by this compassion to identify with a weak disciple (as shown in chapter nine).

For Shinran and for Yuien-bo, the only reason to be religious is to express gratitude for the grace one perceives resulting from Amida's compassion. That compassion is so ultimate that Shinran could exclaim, as he does in chapter one, that there is no good superior to it and no evil that can obstruct it.

Amida's compassion so far exceeds the bounds of our conception that in the epilogue of the *Tannisho* Shinran declares he knew nothing of the meaning of good and evil, for that would be to know good and evil in the depth that Amida knew it.

For our own day, it is essential that we catch Shinran's vision of compassion within ourselves.

CHAPTER 25

The True Nature of Buddha

The final issue of the second section of the *Tannisho*, taken up by Yuien-bo in chapter eighteen, epitomizes the problem running through the entire text: the use of religion as a mask for egoism, in contrast to faith as emancipation from egoism. It is the way of *hakarai*—calculation and self-enhancement, over against the way of reliance on and awareness of the true source and meaning of spiritual power.

Perhaps the best way to illustrate this distinction is found in the story of the woodpecker and the woodcutter. In this ancient story, the woodpecker was quite proud of himself when the tree on which he pecked fell to the ground. In actuality, it was the result of the woodcutter who laid the axe to the root of the tree. Like the woodpecker, the person of self-power has the delusory understanding that what he achieves comes about solely through his individual efforts.

In chapter eighteen the self-power attitude takes an interesting expression. In order to encourage offerings to the fellowship, some Shinshu members advanced the idea that one could become a larger or smaller Buddha in the future depending on the size of one's offerings and donations. Yuien-bo does not waste a moment in declaring this idea as utter nonsense.

Before going into the reasons Yuien-bo offers to demonstrate the error of such a view, we might first consider where such an idea might come from in Shinran's teachings. We are all familiar with the fact that Shinran constantly stressed that we can do nothing to attain enlightenment. The absolute equality of Amida's compassion does not appear to support any idea of graduated reward based on the extent of religious practice. Yet, the idea that was at issue in this chapter must have been set forth as an aspect or possibility in Shinran's teaching, or Yuien-bo would not have had to react to it as one of the confusing issues disturbing the community.

Though Yuien-bo does not himself indicate the source of the idea, we can find a passage in the *Kyogyoshinsho* which may have inspired this wrong view. In the volume on *Transformed Buddha and Transformed Land*, Shinran has taken up the critique of traditional and popular religion. An extensive section relates sutra materials which show that Buddhism is supreme over the folk spirits and gods. Mara and various deities have devoted themselves to the Buddha and will protect believers. Therefore the person with faith is spiritually liberated from the fears and anxieties embodied in popular religious superstitions.

However, in the course of one of these passages in the *Kyogyoshinsho*, directions are given for meditation. The passage concludes:

> If one sincerely meditates and visualizes the Buddha for one day and night to seven days and nights without engaging in any other practices, he will either see a small Buddha with a small (short) meditation and a large Buddha with a large (long) meditation or with an immeasurable meditation, will see infinite Buddha bodies without limit.[1]

In all probability, the massive character of the *Kyogyoshinsho* would make it difficult to distinguish Shinran's personal ideas and comments on the texts he quoted from the quotes themselves, though he prefaces the quotations by indicating that they are such.

However, if a person read carelessly or encountered a lengthy passage, he might consider the idea was Shinran's rather than a quotation by Shinran. Further, in Shinshu tradition, it is assumed generally that what Shinran quoted became his own idea. That is, he quoted it approvingly and thereby made it a part of his teaching. Consequently, enterprising members may have depended upon this passage to encourage other members to make large donations.

Yuien-bo criticizes this effort as using Buddhist teaching to mask worldly desires and to intimidate less affluent and less knowledgeable members. This shows that the advocates of the concept claimed their theory had a basis in Buddhism and in Shinran's teaching.

In refuting the concept that there are degrees of Buddhahood which we attain through religious effort such as donations, Yuien-bo first points out that the true nature of Buddha transcends any suggestion of form, number, size, or color. The *Dharmakaya*, the highest Buddha reality, is purely spiritual. It cannot be subject to human distinctions and categories.

When the Buddha is conceived as the teacher of the Pure Land in the mythology of Buddhism, it is merely a means, correlated to human limitations, in order to help us develop deeper insight into spiritual reality. Thus Shinran stated in the famous *Jinen Honisho*:

> The supreme Buddha is formless, and because of being formless is called *jinen*. When this Buddha is shown as being with form, it is not called the supreme nirvana (Buddha). In order to make us realize that the true Buddha is formless, it is expressly called Amida Buddha; so I have been taught. Amida Buddha is the medium through which we are made to realize *jinen*.[2]

In essence, Shinran and Yuien-bo, following the deeper spiritual insight of Buddhism, emphasize that symbols help us understand life and reality, but we are not to get stuck on the symbol itself. A mark of spiritual and religious maturity is the recognition of the limitations of our religious symbols and concepts, as well as our commitment to their truth.

Yuien-bo goes on to admit that in Buddhist tradition there is the understanding that one may gain a vision of the Buddha as a result of meditation or recitation of the Nembutsu. From Honen's writings we know that such experiences are possible. However, he questions whether such experiences prove that one sees a large or small Buddha depending on whether he recites loudly or softly.

It is interesting to note that the human psychology behind such theories is age-old. It is the principle that more is better. It is common to consider that if something is good, more of it will be better. If something is pleasurable, more would be more pleasurable. Even with medicine, people believe that if it is effective, the effect will increase if one takes more.

However, just the opposite might be true. Too much of a medicine may make it a poison and too much pleasure may turn to boredom. There is also the law of diminishing return. Undoubtedly, Gautama may have been aware of this phenomenon when he taught the Middle Path and avoidance of extremes.

Yuien-bo suggests that to extend these principles of recitation to the practice of donations is to compound the error. If one does have faith, a mind that is true and sincere, to make donations to Buddhas or teachers has no meaning. Conversely, if one has deep faith, it makes no difference what amount one donates.

Against the background of traditional Japanese Buddhism, which had largely been dominated by the nobility, Shinran's teaching liberated Buddhism and the common people from class and economic discrimination in the area of religion. Salvation was no longer a monopoly of the wealthy. Faith was not a matter of competition, economic or spiritual.

For Shinran, and for Yuien-bo, religious practice only has meaning when it leads us beyond our limited conceptions and egoisms to the awareness of spiritual reality which transcends and thus judges our distorted insights.

Once again, in this final chapter of the *Tannisho*, Yuien-bo makes clear the depth of Buddhist spirituality expressed through Shinran's teaching.

CHAPTER **26**

The Mutuality of Interdependence

Essentially, the conflicts Yuien-bo addresses in the second section of the *Tannisho* arose because of differences in the understanding of faith among the followers of Shinran. This problem was not entirely new, as we learn in the first passages of the epilogue to the *Tannisho* where Yuien-bo relates an incident that took place years before, when Shinran was a member of Honen's community at Yoshimizu, before they were all exiled.

At that time, an argument had arisen among the disciples concerning the unity or identity of Shinran's faith and that of their teacher, Honen. Why such a dispute should arise is not clear, but it is possible that Shinran was already, at that time, suggesting some of the distinctive insights that made his later teaching a striking contrast to the Buddhism of his time.

In any case, Shinran—using his former name, Zenshin—maintained that, "Zenshin's faith and Honen Shonin's faith are one." His companion disciples were not satisfied with this view, probably because Shinran implied an unwarranted equality with the teacher Honen. Shinran responded by agreeing that he would be foolish if he claimed that his wisdom and learning were equal to Honen's. However, he went on to indicate that in the matter of ultimate destiny, there could be no difference at all in Shinran's rebirth and that of Honen.

In order to resolve this question, the disciples and Shinran went to Honen for his judgment. Honen agreed with Shinran that faith originates with Amida Buddha. Thus there could be no difference between Honen and Shinran in the outcome of their faith. He also observed that those with different understandings of faith go to different Pure Lands and that, as the dispute revealed, there are those with a different perspective of faith than Shinran.

This incident is interesting, as it reflects discussions and problems within Honen's community at an early time. Similarly, it places the disputes within the early Shinshu community in perspective. The story suggests that questions of faith can be viewed on two levels. On the one hand, there are obvious differences in any social or religious group among the members of that group. There is at least the distinction of leader and follower. People are not all the same; and if they were, it would be a droll, dull world. However, in relation to the deeper aspects of our position in life, there can be no distinction between the leader and the follower. They are all bound together by their common commitment to, and experience of, the reality of Amida's Vow. Honen's and Shinran's faith are equal despite their difference as teacher and disciple because their faith originates from the inspiration of Amida's Original Vow.

In the light of the controversies that divided the early Shinshu community, the insight expressed in this story suggests that all conflicts should be viewed and resolved within the context of faith. On the natural level of life, differences of all sorts are bound to arise and disturb people. There will also be evident differences in ability and attainments. This is the character of finite human life.

Most of our problems arise because our differences with other people appear to outweigh what we have in common with them. Strong awareness of differences is the basis of prejudice in all areas of life. Nevertheless, within the context of faith inspired by Amida's compassionate intention, the fact of difference should never become the standard of judgment or be used as a means for some people to intimidate or dominate others.

Because Shinran's awareness of the all-inclusive compassion of Amida's Vow was stronger than his sense of difference from others, he steadfastly maintained that he was neither a priest nor a layman. He claimed that he had no disciples. He referred to his companions as associates and fellow devotees.

It has been noted that in Shinran's letters he addressed his disciples with honorific terms, showing how highly he respected them. Shinran never allowed the superficial differences between himself and others to limit his recognition of their values and worth as objects of the Buddha's Vow.

All the controversies which Yuien-bo confronted in the second section of the *Tannisho* have the character of setting up a superficial element such as intellectual capacity, moral attainment, or even wealth, as a sign of having proper faith. For Yuien-bo, such considerations completely contradicted the intention of the Vow and distorted Shinran's teaching. It is clear in his teaching that faith does not have its source in human effort or contrivance. Therefore, it cannot be judged by invoking a standard based on human efforts or focusing on natural differences between people.

The implications of this insight for human relations are enormous. Understanding this principle on a deep level would transform the inevitable differences between people from evidences of status and worth to a functional significance that would have value only so far as it enhanced the understanding of faith and deepened the awareness of the reality of the Vow within the world.

As an illustration, we would say that intellectual capacity would only have meaning if it led to deeper appreciation of the faith, and not the exaltation of the person because of his knowledge. Knowledge should be used to deepen faith, not to decorate the person. In the relation of teacher and disciple, the teacher in this view is not superior to the disciple in value or potential. In reality, the only difference between a teacher and a student is that the teacher got there first. The student has the same potential. A teacher is a teacher only by virtue of the human necessity to instruct people and to clarify important issues. The teacher, therefore, is as responsible to the student as the student is to the teacher, as Shinran himself showed in the instance when he disowned his son, Zenran, for abuse of authority.

The deeper root of this mutuality which is the basis for human relations lies in the Primordial, or Original Vow of Amida Buddha. The Vow is the symbol for the mutual interdependence that is the fundamental principle of Mahayana Buddhism.

Were it possible to give a broader social application to this principle in modern society, many of our most severe problems would be more easily solved. Such a perspective enables us to see beyond immediate conflict and differences to the common root in reality we all have. It inspires us to approach issues with respect for the other person, no matter how intense the difference.

When Honen indicates that those with a different faith go to a different Pure Land, he is suggesting that differences in perspective may have different consequences. The resolution of differences requires greater spiritual development, and we must never be complacent in simply accepting differences. We must work them through to unity which expresses the deepest view of the Vow.

When fundamental differences among fellow believers appear, they can only be dealt with by going back to the sources themselves—as Yuien-bo does in the first passages of the epilogue to the *Tannisho* in recounting how Honen's disciples, among whom were Shinran, sought Honen to resolve their question. Yuien-bo's compilation of Shinran's words in the *Tannisho* is a return to sources in order to clarify misunderstandings and resolve differences concerning the teachings of Shinran.

Only in this way can issues be clarified and a true unity of faith realized.

CHAPTER **27**

Expressing What Is True and Real

In the middle portion of the epilogue to the *Tannisho*, Yuien-bo registers his strong desire to make permanent what he had learned from Shinran to serve as a guide for the development of the Shinshu community.

In order to do this, he put into writing a variety of the texts which express Shinran's understanding of the faith. To this task of giving a durable form to the teaching, Yuien-bo contrasts the brevity of his life. In this passage of the epilogue, we gain the impression of a mature Yuien-bo who has accepted transiency as unalterable, and as the basic condition of human life.

We can compare this with Yuien-bo's attitude in chapter nine of the *Tannisho*, where, in his relating an episode from his earlier years, he told how he had reflected to Shinran that he had no joy in the prospect of going to the Pure Land, nor did he desire to go quickly—despite its glory depicted in the sutras.

We cannot expect that youth would easily give up the joy of vitality. However, as years wear on, we become more and more aware, as in Yuien-bo's description of the epilogue, that our lives are like dewdrops on a withered blade of grass. Hardly anything could express fragility and impermanence more acutely than this.

Despite these limitations on his life, Yuien-bo dedicated himself in these waning years of his life to listening to the questions and doubts of his fellow-believers, and sharing with them what he had learned from Shinran. In addition to this verbal sharing, he took up his brush to record the result of these dialogues and exchanges, together with perhaps less than one-hundredth of all that he had heard Shinran say regarding the teachings.

It is difficult to express the wondrous event that has taken place here. Though we are impermanent, it is possible through writing to communicate in a measure with later times, as the *Tannisho* communicates to us over a time gap of more than seven hundred years.

In our present age, we emphasize communication between living persons in dialogue. This is a wondrous event also. However, we can relate to the generations of the past and the generations of the future only through written or recorded words.

In our present time, there has been a scorn of books and of the written word because of disillusion with intellectual endeavor, as well as because of the prominence of visual media. When we observe censorship, or book burning, we can sense the importance of the written word. What is altered, or what is destroyed, cuts us off from a valuable heritage.

Without the words which Yuien-bo has left us in the *Tannisho*, we could not touch the mind of Shinran as intimately as we do across that time gap of more than seven hundred years. Without the written word, we would indeed not have the treasures from all areas of culture that are available through the texts left to us.

I believe we would have fewer reading problems among our schoolchildren if we could convey to them the sense of wonder and the real privilege there is in being able to read, and in so doing having the ages at our fingertips. To depreciate "book learning" is to narrow the potentialities of our own existence.

Today, there is a great hesitancy to express ourselves in writing. As the editor of a small paper, I constantly receive the refrain: "I can't write."

What would we have missed if Yuien-bo had feared to take up the brush? The propagation of a faith through written texts is essential to maintain the vitality and meaning of that faith through the changing conditions of the world. That many reformers return to the *Tannisho* in order to find inspiration and meaning in Shinshu for their time is evidence of the importance of this.

Yuien-bo states that he had listened to the followers and shared with them what he learned from Shinran. What stands out in this important statement in the epilogue is the fact that Yuien-bo listened to the followers. We naturally think that followers should listen to the teacher. However, the teacher cannot really be a teacher unless he also listens to his students and knows their problems or the gaps in their understanding.

Yuien-bo's reflections are important for the whole problem of leadership. The best leader does not separate from the people but keeps in close touch personally with their lives. The vividness and spiritual impact of the *Tannisho* is directly the result of the fact that Yuien-bo directed his thought to real problems in the Shinshu community. He was a good listener, and thereby a good teacher.

In line with his desire to maintain the faith after he has departed from this life, Yuien-bo encourages the disciples to also consult the many scriptures which Shinran had used as support for his interpretation of Buddhism. Shinran had copied numerous texts during his later years in Kyoto, which he sent to the disciples in the Mito-Kanto area to help them understand the issues of Pure Land teaching. He had also composed texts and anthologies which give the basis for his teaching.

Yuien-bo, in the epilogue to the *Tannisho*, asks followers to become as widely knowledgeable as they can in the teachings of Shinran. In earlier discussions, Yuien-bo made it abundantly clear that salvation is not achieved by the accumulation of knowledge. However, he has also made it clear that problems can be avoided and resolved when there is an understanding of the teaching and its basis in Buddhist tradition. Ignorance never solved problems.

In consulting the texts and scriptures that are the foundation of Shinshu, they are to be read critically. Yuien-bo was wise enough to recognize, as Shinran had done before him, that books alone are not entirely sufficient. They must be understood and interpreted.

Mahayana Buddhism from its very beginnings recognized the variety of levels of understanding in receiving the Buddha's teaching. Thus in the history of Buddhism there developed the procedure known as critical classification of doctrines. This method aimed to bring order to the diversity of Buddhist teachings, and to determine the true way to enlightenment. It had not merely theoretical concerns, but practical concerns in establishing the central practice of Buddhism, depending on the school in question.

Shinran also formulated a system of his own to demonstrate the importance of *shinjin*, the true and real mind, and Other Power Nembutsu. A fundamental distinction used by Shinran was the categories of true and real versus provisional and temporary. In our study of Shinshu, we must always strive to determine the true and real beyond the provisional and temporary. Thus Yuien-bo emphasizes the critical approach this implies when he declares, "The Shonin intended that we should abandon the expedient and keep the real, set aside the temporary and follow the true."

In the light of this passage in the epilogue, Yuien-bo had gathered together the first and second sections of the *Tannisho* to serve as a guide to the spirit of Shinran and as a norm to measure the various teachings set forth in the name of scripture or Buddhist tradition, and claiming to be the true way.

In the *Kyogyoshinsho* Shinran had made an important distinction concerning the levels of teachings which made it possible for him to unify Pure Land tradition, while at the same time showing its diversity. There was an explicit and implicit aspect to each stage in the evolution of the teaching.

In relation to the sutras, they advocate in the explicit aspect the recitation of the Nembutsu as a way of cultivating roots of goodness and virtue. In their implicit aspect, the sutras "disclose the inconceivable ocean-like Vow with a view to leading the sentient beings to the sea of unhindered Great Faith."[1]

We learn from this passage the importance of commitment and concern for the preservation of the unity of faith and the continuity of the teaching. Because of Yuien-bo's commitment, his concern, and keenness of mind, we can now enjoy the continuity of Shinran's teachings in the spiritual classic, the *Tannisho.*

Now, we, too, must also take up Yuien-bo's task in bringing to our study of Shinshu the critical perspective and knowledge required. We must keep close to people, and be guided by the spirit of Shinran in discovering the most profound way to realize and to express compassion in our fragmented world.

CHAPTER 28

The Light of Limitless Compassion

Yuien-bo concludes the epilogue, and the *Tannisho*, with two final quotations of Shinran that are a crescendo of faith and spirituality. These two passages, rather than being a proclamation of doctrine or formal teaching, reveal Shinran's perspective on the nature of faith.

In the first passage, Shinran is quoted as exclaiming joyously that when he reflected on Amida's great effort through five kalpas in establishing the Vows, he realized it had all been done for Shinran alone.

The second declaration attributed to Shinran contrasts our knowledge of good and evil and hence the limited nature of human judgment when compared with the absoluteness of Amida Buddha. We can only claim to know what is good or evil when we know it as Amida knows it through his efforts in realizing perfect goodness.

The standard of perfection symbolized in Amida Buddha renders all human pretentions lies and deceits. According to Shinran, only the Nembutsu is true as the reflection and expression of Amida's truth and sincerity in the world.

It is interesting that Yuien-bo places these quotations after his distinctions of doctrine into true and provisional, and the statements by Shinran which act as guides in determining judgments on doctrinal matters. In these final passages of the epilogue, Yuien-bo is pressing deeper and placing all issues and arguments in their proper perspective.

For Shinran, faith is not a matter of texts, distinctions, or arguments, however sagelike those texts, distinctions, or arguments might be. Faith is, rather, his deep awareness, based on his personal experience, that what is essential is the lively, inner awareness of Amida's compassion. He lets us know that faith is deeply personal, and whatever truth or reality we claim to follow, that truth or reality must be experienced as our own.

Shinran's assertion that it was all done for Shinran alone was not meant to be a selfish or arrogant claim that he had a monopoly on Amida's compassion. Shinran could not so easily cast aside the long tradition of Buddhist pursuit of egolessness, nor his own awareness that he was, after all, a passion-ridden human being, grasping after fame and power as are all other human beings. Rather, Shinran's declaration here must be viewed in the light of the Buddhist teaching of interdependence and mutual identity, major Mahayana principles that underlie Shinran's teaching as they do other Mahayana schools.

Here, Shinran is at once himself and all other beings. He is the focal point where reality becomes expressed. His reality is the reality of all things, and all things are his reality. The limitless compassion of Amida is as fully given to others as it is to Shinran, just as a light spreads equally in all directions from its source. Amida embraces Shinran and all others equally. However, the reality of that universal compassion must be experienced in its totality within the individual consciousness of the person. If it is not first perceived in one's consciousness, it has no meaning as an abstraction or as a doctrine.

In probing his own inner life, Shinran was perhaps one of the most subjective of Buddhist teachers. Though he perceived himself as a karma-bound and passion-ridden being, the warmth of Amida's compassion melted all obstructions and anxieties concerning his future destiny and the meaning of his life.

Although we each experience our faith in various ways, Shinran is indicating to us that vital and meaningful faith is not so much a question of belief in abstract doctrines and systems, or of organization and traditions, as it is a personal involvement and identification with the realities symbolized in the teaching. Tradition and awareness are interrelated and interdependent. They are the true foundation of religious community.

Shinran points us toward the absoluteness of Amida, whose truth reveals the limited and deceptive nature of purely human judgments. In this final statement attributed to Shinran by Yuien-bo, his pessimism about the vanity of the world—which he describes as a burning house, impermanent, delusive, and deceptive—rests on the firm realization that the Nembutsu, as the manifestation of Amida's compassion, is the only truth, the only reality.

Shinran is not resigned to despair or hopelessness. Like Shotoku Taishi in an earlier age in Japan (who declared that all the world is false and only the Buddha is true), Shinran was able to negate the world, and thereby relate more creatively to it, as he perceived its true reality through the Vow of Amida. The darkness of delusion was banished by the light of Amida's truth. Though many consider religion and faith as unrealistic, Shinran here reveals that religion is realistic, because it banishes delusions about ourselves and the world we live in and create.

In our social and religious communities we may argue and conflict for many reasons. Everyone attempts to justify themselves in order to maintain their self-esteem and superiority over the other. In modern terms, Shinran recognized that we all play games for our own advantage. However, there is one truth which he declared from beginning to end: the compassion of Amida's embrace.

This was not merely a doctrine or a system. It was a living experience which reveals the shallowness of our egoistic, religious pretentions. If we measure our deeds by the standard of Amida's work, even our best intentions fall short.

Awareness of our true situation opens us to deeper relations and unity with our fellows. We seek the profound meaning of compassion in spite of our differences.

The *Tannisho* begins with the Vow whose realization is the source of our spiritual life, and it ends with the Vow as the standard for all our dealings in life. The final sentence of the epilogue, in which Yuien-bo warns that this text must not be shown to outsiders, is perhaps a political warning for those times when Shinshu was not approved by the powers of government or of traditional Buddhism, and its followers were liable to persecution because of their beliefs.

Essentially, the epilogue ends with the Vow as the standard for all our dealings in life. The unity of the fellowship must be founded on a deep and personal awareness of the compassion expressed in the Vow, and not on human considerations. Through all the issues that Yuien-bo presents in the *Tannisho*, we can observe the ongoing struggle (then as now) to make real the broad spirit of the Vow for living and human fellowship in the face of human tendencies to narrow the boundaries of community and to exalt the self.

In these twenty-eight chapters, we have by no means exhausted the richness of this text, but merely hope that we have contributed a little to its understanding and meaning for today. Hanada sensei of Nagoya said, "Just as a painting needs a canvas on which the painting can be drawn, so too the words of the *Tannisho* need a canvas—your life, my life—on which it can be drawn. Only then, on the canvas of our life, does the *Tannisho* become truly meaningful."[1]

NAMU AMIDA BUTSU!

Notes

2. About Yuien-bo

1. There are several theories concerning the identity of Yuien-bo, but it is not the purpose of this essay to analyze those suggestions. Readers might refer to the recent work of Shigematsu Akihisa, *Chusei shinshu shiso no kenkyu* (Tokyo: Yoshikawa kobunkan, 1973), 84–106.

4. Faith and Reality

1. F. Max Muller, ed., *Sacred Books of the East*, LXIX (London: Oxford University Press, 1894), 180.

2. Shinran, *The Kyo Gyo Shin Sho: The Teaching, Practice, Faith, and Enlightenment*, Ryukoku Translation Series, V (Kyoto: Ryukoku University, 1966), 113–4.

3. Ibid., 132.

4. Ibid., 211.

7. The Transformation of Faith

1. *The Kyo Gyo Shin Sho*, Ryukoku Translation Series, 107.

2. *Shinshu Shogyo Zensho*, II (Kyoto: Kokyo-shoin, 1957), 697. Hereafter referred to as *SSZ*. Author's translation.

9. Buddhist Views of Morality

1. *SSZ*, II, 195–6.

2. Ibid., 196. Author's translation.

11. The Way of No-Hindrance

1. Gutoku Shaku Shinran, *The Kyogyoshinsho: The Collection of Passages Expounding the True Teaching, Living, Faith, and Realizing of the Pure Land*, trans. D. T. Suzuki (Kyoto: Shinshu Otaniha, 1973), 68; *SSZ*, II, 39.

2. Ibid., 64; *SSZ*, II, 36.
3. *Mattosho*, III in *SSZ*, II, 661. Author's translation.
4. *SSZ*, II, 656. Author's translation.

13. The Revolutionary Reality of the Nembutsu

1. Shinran, *Letters of Shinran: A Translation of Mattosho*, ed. Yoshifumi Ueda, Shin Buddhism Translation Series, I (Kyoto: Hongwanji International Center, 1978), 39–40.

14. The Affirmation of Doubt

1. *Shinshu Seiten*, ed. Tri-State Buddhist Temples (San Francisco: Buddhist Churches of America, 1978), 14.
2. *The Kyo Gyo Shin Sho*, Ryukoku Translation Series, 132.
3. Ibid., 118.
4. Takie S. Lebra and William P. Lebra, *Japanese Culture and Behavior* (Honolulu: University of Hawaii, 1974), 431.

17. The Issue of Vow and Name

1. *Letters of Shinran*, ed. Yoshifumi Ueda, 37.
2. Dennis Hirota, "Ichigon Hodan," *Eastern Buddhist* New Series IX–1 (May 1977): 128.
3. *The Kyo Gyo Shin Sho*, Ryukoku Translation Series, 112.

25. The True Nature of Buddha

1. *SSZ*, II, 178. Author's translation.
2. *Letters of Shinran*, ed. Yoshifumi Ueda, 30.

27. Expressing What Is True and Real

1. *The Kyo Gyo Shin Sho*, Ryukoku Translation Series, 186–7.

28. The Light of Limitless Compassion

1. Masao Hanada, *Living Shin Buddhism* (Honolulu: Buddhist Study Center, 1978), 11.

Glossary

Accomplishing Vow.
> The twentieth of the Forty-eight Vows made by the Bodhi-sattva Dharmakara. In this Vow, Dharmakara says that those sentient beings who, having heard his Name, desire to be born in his land and sincerely turn their merits towards that goal, shall be born there. Shinran believed that although the sentient beings described in the Twentieth Vow still depend upon their own abilities, doubting Amida's power, they will eventually attain birth in the Pure Land because Amida promised to accomplish their salvation in the Twentieth Vow. *See* "Forty-Eight Vows."

Amida.
> The Japanese term for the Buddha Amitabha ("Infinite Light") or the Buddha Amitayus ("Infinite Life"). When the Bodhi-sattva Dharmakara (Jpn. Hozo Bosatsu) fulfilled his Forty-eight Vows, he became a Buddha by this name and took up residence in his Pure Land in the Western quarter. The name "Infinite Light" symbolizes his infinite wisdom, while the name "Infinite Life" symbolizes his infinite compassion.

Amida's Vow.
> *See* "Original Vow."

Amitayus ("Infinite Life").
> *See* "Amida."

Arhat ("one who has killed the enemy, i.e., evil passions" or "one who is worthy of offerings").
> One who has attained the highest stage of the Hinayana. An arhat has eradicated all evil passions and attained liberation from samsara.

Assembly of the Truly Assured.
> The third of these three types of people:

1) Wrongly Established Ones: These people rely upon their own abilities when they perform their various religious practices to achieve birth in the Pure Land. They are the people described in the Nineteenth Vow of the Bodhisattva Dharmakara.

2) Indeterminate Ones: Although these people practice the Nembutsu, the practice made possible by Other Power, they do not have true faith and continue to depend on their own abilities. Thus they attain imperfect liberation. These are the people described in the Twentieth Vow of the Bodhisattva Dharmakara.

3) Truly Assured Ones: These people practice the Nembutsu with true faith in Amida. They are assured of birth in the Pure Land and attainment of enlightenment. These are the people described in the Eighteenth Vow of the Bodhisattva Dharmakara.

Birth (in the Pure Land).

In the Pure Land tradition, practitioners seek rebirth in the Pure Land after death so that they can attain enlightenment in the Pure Land. In contrast, other Buddhist traditions talk about attaining enlightenment in this world.

Bodhisattva ("Seeker of Enlightenment").

This term originally referred to Shakyamuni before he attained enlightenment. In Mahayana Buddhism, it came to mean any seeker of enlightenment.

Bodhisattva Dharmakara (Jpn. Hozo Bosatsu).

Dharmakara ("Storehouse of the Dharma") is the name of the hero of the *Larger Sukhavativyuha-sutra*. He makes Forty-eight Vows to become a Buddha. After long practice, he fulfills his vows and becomes a Buddha by the name of Amitabha or Amitayus. *See* "Amida," "Forty-Eight Vows," *and* "Nembutsu."

Body of Recompense.

See "Transformed (Buddha) Body."

Borderland.

Another name for the Transformed (Buddha) Land. The land of imperfect liberation where those who rely on their own abilities and doubt Amida's power are reborn. It is contrasted with the Land of Recompense, the sphere of perfect liberation where those with true faith are reborn. *See* "Transformed Land" *and* "Land of Recompense."

Buddha ("Awakened One").
As a proper noun, this means Gautama or Shakyamuni. As a common noun, it means any awakened person. *See* "Shakyamuni."

Castle of Doubt.
The place of imperfect liberation where those who doubt Amida's power are reborn.

Chigi (Chih-i, A.D. 538–97).
The founder of the Chinese T'ien-t'ai school. *See* "Tendai."

Compassion (Jpn. *jihi*).
The word *jihi* consists of two terms: *ji* (Skt. *maitri*) and *hi* (Skt. *karuna*). *Ji* means "affection" or "the desire to give comfort to others." *Hi* means "pity" or "sympathy for those who suffer and desire to end their suffering." Compassion and wisdom are two of the most important virtues in Mahayana Buddhism.

Dhammapada (*Taisho Shinshu Daizokyo* [hereafter abbreviated as *T.*] vol. 4, pp. 559–799).
One of the earliest Buddhist texts, the *Dhammapada* consists of sayings attributed to Shakyamuni Buddha. It is in the Pali language, and is part of the sutra canon of the Theravada school.

Dharma ("Law" or "Principle").
The truth taught by Buddhism—the truth of impermanence, selflessness, emptiness, and dependent origination.

Dharmakara.
See "Bodhisattva Dharmakara."

Dharmakaya.
See "Transformed Body."

Donran (T'an-luan, A.D. 476–542).
The third of the seven patriarchs of the Shin Buddhist school. His main work is the *Ojoron-chu* (*T.* vol. 40, pp. 826–43), a commentary on Vasubandhu's *Pure Land Treatise. See* "Other Power" *and* "Vasubandhu."

Easy Practice.
Nembutsu practice (recitation of the name of Amida Buddha), i.e., saying *Namu Amida Butsu*. Such recitation is called "easy

161

practice," because it enables those of inferior potential to attain birth in the Pure Land. It is contrasted with "difficult practice," religious practices which those of superior potential perform to attain Buddhahood in this life. The doctrinal classifications "easy practice" and "difficult practice" were originally formulated by Nagarjuna (ca. A.D. 150–250) in the "Chapter on Easy Practice" in his *Dasabhumi-vibhasa-sastra.* (*T.* vol. 26, pp. 40–4.)

Eighteenth Vow.

One of the Forty-eight Vows which the Bodhisattva Dharmakara made. It says, "When I have attained Buddhahood, all the sentient beings of the ten quarters will be of sincere mind, have serene faith, and wish to be born in my country. If they are not born there even after meditating on me up to ten times, may I not attain perfect enlightenment. But I exclude those who have committed the five deadly sins and abused the right Dharma."

Eightfold Noble Path.

According to the Buddha, the path that leads to the cessation of suffering. The practitioner must develop: 1) right view, 2) right thought, 3) right speech, 4) right action, 5) right livelihood, 6) right effort, 7) right mindfulness, and 8) right meditation.

Eighty Secondary Features of (a Buddha).

The eighty minor characteristics accompanying the thirty-two major marks of a Buddha.

Eko (Skt. *parinama*, "transfer").

There is a considerable difference between the Jodo Shinshu and other Buddhist traditions in their interpretation of *eko*. In the Jodo Shinshu, sentient beings' salvation depends totally on the merit which Amida transfers to them, not on the merit which sentient beings themselves accumulate. Sentient beings cannot, in this life, transfer their merit to other people to benefit them. In other Buddhist traditions, sentient beings can, in this life, attain enlightenment through the merit they have accumulated and can transfer their merit to other people to benefit them.

Enlightenment (Skt. *bodhi*, "awakening").

When, at the age of thirty-five, Shakyamuni recognized the truth of things-as-they-really-are, he experienced enlightenment and became a Buddha.

Eshinni (A.D. 1182–1268).
    Shinran's wife. *See* "Shinran."

Evil Person.
    In Shin Buddhism, one is supposed to identify oneself as "an evil person"—a person who is incapable of performing virtuous actions and is constantly committing evil actions. "An evil person" is the primary object of Amida's compassion. *See* "Good Person."

Expedient Means (Skt. *upaya*).
    The ingenious methods by which a Buddha or Bodhisattva, out of compassion, teaches sentient beings and guides them to the Dharma.

Faith (Jpn. *shinjin*).
    Faith in Amida Buddha. In Shin Buddhism, faith is the only precondition for birth in the Pure Land and is entirely a gift from Amida. Shinran says that when one has true faith, one cannot help reciting the Nembutsu, the verbal expression of faith. Faith is accompanied by a feeling of joy and gratitude. *See* "Nembutsu."

Final Dharma.
    See "*Mappo*."

Five Deadly Sins.
    Traditionally considered the five sins which cannot be forgiven. However, Shinran believed that he was guilty of them all and that Amida accepted him anyway. The five deadly sins are: 1) patricide, 2) matricide, 3) killing an arhat, 4) maliciously causing a Buddha to bleed, and 5) causing disharmony in the Sangha.

Forty-Eight Vows.
    The vows made by the Bodhisattva Dharmakara in the *Larger Sukhavativyuha-sutra*. In these vows Dharmakara expressed his desire to create a Buddha land (or Pure Land) for all sentient beings. *See* "Eighteenth Vow" *and* "Accomplishing Vow."

Four Modes of Birth.
    Traditionally believed to be the four possible ways that a being may be born. They are: 1) birth from a womb, 2) birth from an egg, 3) birth from moisture, and 4) birth by metamorphosis.

Four Practices for the Attainment of Happiness.
    A set of Buddhist practices recommended in the *Lotus Sutra* but disparaged as "self-power" practices in the *Tannisho*. They are:

1) disciplining the actions of the body, 2) disciplining the words of the mouth, 3) disciplining thoughts, and 4) vowing to preach the *Lotus Sutra* to all sentient beings.

Four Vows of the Bodhisattva.

The vows which a Bodhisattva (seeker of Buddhahood) makes at the outset of his practice. They are: 1) Though there are an infinite number of sentient beings, I vow to save them all; 2) Though there are an infinite number of passions, I vow to sever them all; 3) Though there are an infinite number of doctrines, I vow to know them all; and 4) The Buddhist path being supreme, I vow to attain it. On the basis of these four vows, Bodhisattvas such as Dharmakara made their specific vows. *See* "Forty-Eight Vows."

Gautama.

Siddhartha Gautama is the name of the historical Buddha. *See* "Buddha" *and* "Shakyamuni."

Good Person.

In Shin Buddhism, one is supposed to identify oneself as "an evil person." One who considers himself good or capable of performing virtuous actions is not the primary object of Amida's compassion. *See* "Evil Person."

Good Teacher (Skt. *kalyanamitra*, "good friend").

One who guides people in their spiritual development in the Dharma.

Hell.

The lowest of the six realms of mortal existence in ancient Indian cosmology. *See* "Six Realms of Mortal Existence."

Holy Path.

See "Path of the Sages."

Honen (A.D. 1133–1212).

The founder of the Japanese Pure Land (or Jodo) School. He was born in Kume in Mimasaka Province (the present Okayama Prefecture). At the age of fifteen, he went to Mt. Hiei, where he studied the Tendai doctrine under eminent monks. At forty-three, when he was desperately seeking the way to liberation, he discovered the writings of Zendo (Shan-tao, A.D. 613–81), a Chinese Pure Land teacher. After that he considered himself a follower of Zendo and practiced the Nembutsu exclusively. He left Mt. Hiei and lived in Yoshimizu, where he propagated the Nembutsu among people from all walks of life. In 1198, at the request of Fujiwara Kanezane, the lord chancellor, he composed the *Senjaku-hongan-nembutsu-shu* (Treatise on the Nembutsu of the Select Original Vow), whose publication marked the founding of the Japanese Pure Land School. In 1206, his school was persecuted by the authorities and he was exiled to Tosa in Shikoku. In 1212, one year after he was pardoned and came back to Kyoto, he died. *See "Zendo" and "Senjaku-shu."*

Hozo.

   See "Bodhisattva Dharmakara."

Ignorance (Skt. *avidya*).

   This is the basic cause of suffering and hinders gaining insight into the Buddha's wisdom. It takes two forms, wrong beliefs and absence of wisdom. Ignorance, greed, and anger are called "the three poisons."

Ikko ("Single-minded").

   Refers to single-minded and exclusive practice of the Nembutsu. Ikko-shu ("Single-minded School") is another designation for the Jodo Shinshu.

Ippen (A.D. 1239–89).

   The founder of the Ji school, a Pure Land school in Japan.

Jinen.

   See "Naturalness and Spontaneity."

Jodo Shinshu ("True Pure Land School").

   Otherwise called the Shinshu or Shin Buddhism. For Shinran, the term "Jodo Shinshu" meant "true Pure Land teaching" and designated the teachings of Honen. After Shinran's death it became the name of the school Shinran founded.

Kalpa.

   An "aeon" or "immeasurably long period of time." There are four types of kalpas: small, medium, great, and incalculable.

Karma.

   Any action of the body, mouth, or mind. Since most actions have a good or evil effect on a person's character and determine the nature of his future existence, the concept came to be connected with the Buddhist theory of transmigration. *See* "Samsara."

Kegon Sutra (Skt. *Avatamsaka-sutra*, *T.* vol. 9, pp. 395–788).
The basic text of the Kegon (or Hua-yen) school.

Kukai (otherwise known as Kobo-daishi, A.D. 774–835).
The founder of the Shingon school in Japan.

Kyogyoshinsho ("Teaching, Practice, Faith, and Attainment").
The abridged title of the main work of Shinran (A.D. 1173–1262), the founder of Shin Buddhism. The full title is *Ken-jodo-shinjitsu-kyogyosho-monrui* (A Collection of Passages Concerning Teaching, Practice, and Attainment, Which Reveal the Truth of the Pure Land). It is in six fascicles. (*T.* vol. 83, pp. 589–644). *See* "Shinran."

Land of Recompense.
Another name for the Pure Land which Amida Buddha created by fulfilling his Forty-eight Vows. The word "recompense" means that it is a "recompense (or reward)" for his vows and practice. This is the realm where those who have true faith are reborn. *See* "Transformed Land" *and* "Borderland."

Land of Sloth and Pride.
The land of imperfect liberation where arrogant people who cannot accept Amida's Vow are born. Because these people think themselves important and do not seek the way diligently, they are lax in their practice.

Larger Pure Land Sutra.
See "*Larger Sukhavativyuha-sutra.*"

Larger Sukhavativyuha-sutra.
Shinran considered this text to be the basis of his Buddhist views. There are five extant Chinese translations of this sutra. The translation made by Sanghavarman in A.D. 252 (*T.* vol. 12, pp. 265–79) became one of the three sutras which make up the so-called triple sutra of the Pure Land school.

Lotus Sutra (Skt. *Saddharma-pundarika-sutra*).
One of the most popular Mahayana sutras in China and Japan, this sutra became the basic text of the Tendai and Nichiren sects. Several partial or complete translations were made from

Sanskrit to Chinese, and the one translated by Kumarajiva in 406 (*T.* vol. 9, pp. 1–62) became the most popular.

Mahayana ("Larger Vehicle").

A form of Buddhism which appeared in India around 100 B.C. and which exalted as its religious ideal the Bodhisattva, the great being who is willing to delay his own enlightenment until he can save all sentient beings. Such selfless compassion becomes possible only when the practitioner grasps the central Mahayana doctrine of *sunyata* ("emptiness") and so realizes that "himself" and "others" are not separate as we usually believe. Mahayanists called their opponents' belief system "the Hinayana (Lesser Vehicle)," alleging that its adherents were only interested in their own personal salvation. Today most of the Buddhists in Nepal, Tibet, China, Mongolia, Vietnam, Bhutan, Korea, and Japan are Mahayanists.

Mantra.

See "Three Mystic Practices."

Mappo ("Final Dharma [Period]").

The third of the following three periods:

1) True Dharma Period: During this period (the first five hundred years after the passing of the Buddha, according to one theory) all three essentials of Buddhism, true teaching, true practice, and true enlightenment, existed.

2) Image Dharma Period: During this period (which lasted a thousand years, according to one theory) both true teaching and true practice still existed, but no one became enlightened.

3) Final Dharma Period: During this period (which will last ten thousand years) the true teaching alone is still alive; neither true practice nor true enlightenment exist. Even the true teaching will gradually disappear.

Mara.

The demon who hinders Buddhist practice.

Mattosho (*T.* vol. 83, pp. 711–22).

A collection of twenty-two of Shinran's letters, all written when Shinran was 79 to 88.

Meditation Sutra (Skt. *Amitayurdhyana-sutra*, *T.* vol. 12, pp. 340–6).

Tradition says that this sutra was translated into Chinese during the Yuan-chia period (A.D. 424–53) by Kalayasas, a monk from central Asia. It is one of the three sutras which make up the so-called triple sutra of the Pure Land school.

Mt. Hiei.

A mountain located between Kyoto and Shiga Prefecture. In 787 Saicho (A.D. 767–822), the founder of the Japanese Tendai school, built the first temple of that school on this mountain. Thereafter it was one of the main centers of Buddhist learning in Japan. Many Buddhist teachers of the Kamakura period (A.D. 1185–1332), notably Honen, Shinran, Dogen, Eisai, and Nichiren, originally studied there.

Mudra.

See "Three Mystic Practices."

Myokonin ("a lay saint").

One who devoutly practices the Nembutsu.

Name.

The so-called six-character name of Amida Buddha, which is *Namu Amida Butsu*. Recitation of this name is called the Nembutsu or *shomyo* (name-calling). *See* "Nembutsu."

Namu Amida Butsu ("I take refuge in Amida Buddha").

See "Name" *and* "Nembutsu."

Naturalness and Spontaneity (Jpn. *jinen*).

The working of Amida's power, which is beyond human understanding.

Nembutsu (Skt. *Buddha-anusmrti*, "recollection of the Buddha").

Recitation of Amida's name, i.e., *Namu Amida Butsu*. In his Eighteenth Vow, the Bodhisattva Dharmakara says that he will save those of inferior capacity, those who are only capable of meditating on him up to ten times. Zendo (Shan-tao, A.D. 613–81) interpreted "meditating ten times" to mean "reciting Amida's name ten times"—a practice for the most inferior type of person. On the basis of this interpretation of Shan-tao, Japanese Pure Land masters like Honen and Shinran developed their doctrines. *See* "Eighteenth Vow," "Shinran," *and* "Honen."

Nembutsu-bo (otherwise known as Nen Amida Butsu, A.D. 1156–1251).

A disciple of Honen.

Nichiren (A.D. 1222–82).

The founder of the Nichiren school.

Non-retrogression (Skt. *avinivartaniya*).

In traditional Mahayana doctrine, this is often identified as the first stage of Bodhisattvahood, the stage in which a Bodhisattva will no longer fall back to lower stages. According to Shinran, the moment one's faith in Amida Buddha is firmly established, one enters this stage and never slides back. Those who have entered this stage are called the "Assembly of the Truly Assured." *See* "Assembly of the Truly Assured."

One Vehicle (Skt. *eka-yana*).

The doctrine, otherwise known as the Buddha vehicle, which is described in such sutras as the *Lotus Sutra*. According to the *Lotus Sutra*, the One Vehicle is the ultimate teaching of the Buddha, although the Buddha taught three other types of teachings (i.e., the Sravaka vehicle, the Pratyeka-buddha vehicle, and the Bodhisattva vehicle) as expedient means to guide all sentient beings to the One Vehicle.

Original Vow (Skt. *purva-pranidhana*).

The Forty-eight Vows which the Bodhisattva Dharmakara made to save all sentient beings. In these vows he expressed his desire to create a Pure Land for all sentient beings. This term sometimes refers specifically to the Eighteenth Vow, in which Dharmakara says that he will save even those with very inferior potential. *See* "Forty-Eight Vows" *and* "Eighteenth Vow."

Other Power.

The power of Amida's vow to save all sentient beings. This term is contrasted with self-power (or self effort), which means the religious efforts of a practitioner who relies on his own abilities. These two categories, "Other Power" and "self-power" were originally formulated by Donran (T'an-luan, A.D. 476–542), the third patriarch of the Jodo Shinshu, in his commentary on Vasubandhu's (ca. A.D. 330–400) *Sukhavati-vyuha-upadesa* (*T.* vol. 40, pp. 844 a). They were T'an-luan's reformulation of Nagarjuna's (ca. A.D. 150–250) categories, "Easy Practice" and "Difficult Practice." *See* "Easy Practice."

Paramita (Perfection) of Giving.

> The first of the six *paramita*s, the perfect virtues which are practiced by a Bodhisattva. They are: 1) perfect giving, 2) keeping the precepts perfectly, 3) perfect patience, 4) perfect effort, 5) perfect meditation, and 6) perfect wisdom.

Passions (Skt. *klesa*, "defilement").

> Mental functions such as greed, anger, and ignorance, which disturb and distress one's mind and body. They cause one to transmigrate through the cycle of birth and death.

Path of the Sages.

> The path by which one can attain enlightenment in this life. This is contrasted with the Pure Land path, in which one attains birth in the Pure Land after death through the power of Amida Buddha's Vow. These two paths were originally formulated by Doshaku (Tao-ch'o, A.D. 562–645), a Chinese Pure Land monk, in his *Anraku-shu* (*T.* vol. 47, pp. 4–22). "The path of the sages" is synonymous with "difficult practice," or "self-power." *See* "Easy Practice" *and* "Other Power."

Precepts (Skt. *sila*).

> Vows concerning daily conduct taken by lay Buddhists and monks. There are five precepts for lay Buddhists and two hundred and fifty for fully ordained monks.

Pure Land (Skt. *Sukhavati*, "possessing bliss").

> The name of the Buddha land in the Western quarter, which was created by the Bodhisattva Dharmakara when he became Amida Buddha. *See* "Utmost Bliss."

Pure Land Path.

> The path on which one attains birth in the Pure Land after death through the power of Amida Buddha. This path is synonymous with "Easy Practice," or "Other Power." *See* "Path of the Sages."

Pure Land Treatise (Skt. *Sukhavativyuha-sutra-upadesa, T.* vol. 26, pp. 230–3).

> Written by Vasubandhu (ca. A.D. 300–400), an Indian Mahayana master who was regarded as the second Pure Land patriarch by Shinran. This text was translated into Chinese early in the sixth century by Bodhiruci, a monk from northern India. The main work of Donran (T'an-luan, A.D. 476–542), the third patriarch of Jodo Shinshu, is a commentary on this text.

Rebirth (in the Pure Land).
>   *See* "Birth."

Recitation (of the Name).
>   *See* "Name" *and* "Nembutsu."

Recompense.
>   *See* "Land of Recompense" *and* "Transformed Body."

Rennyo (A.D. 1414–99).
>   The eighth abbot of the Shinshu, he is known as the restorer of the Shin Buddhist tradition. His disciples compiled a collection of his sayings called the *Goichidai-kikigaki* (Records of Rennyo's Talks) (*T.* vol. 83, pp. 809–32). The *Ofumi* (or *Gobunsho*) is a collection of his letters in five fascicles (*T.* vol. 83, pp. 771–808).

Rightly Established State.
>   *See* "Assembly of the Truly Assured."

Sage Path.
>   *See* "Path of the Sages."

Saicho (otherwise known as Dengyo-daishi, A.D. 767–822).
>   The founder of the Tendai school in Japan.

Samsara.
>   "Transmigration" or "the cycle of birth and death." Because of karmic causes, sentient beings transmigrate within the six realms of mortal existence. The Buddha's teachings are designed to liberate sentient beings from samsara, which is generally contrasted with nirvana or enlightenment. *See* "Karma" *and* "Six Realms of Mortal Existence."

Seikan-bo (otherwise known as Genchi, A.D. 1182–1238).
>   A disciple of Honen who wrote the *Senjaku Yoketsu*, the *Kogi Zuiketsu-shu*, and other works.

Self-Power.
>   The religious efforts of a practitioner who relies on his own abilities. *See* "Other Power."

Senjaku-shu (*T.* vol. 83, pp. 1–20).
>   The abridged name of the *Senjaku-hongan-nembutsu-shu* (A Treatise on the Nembutsu of the Select Original Vow). This is the main work of Honen (A.D. 1133–1212), the founder of the Japanese Pure Land (Jodo) school. *See* "Honen."

Sentient Beings (Skt. *sattva*).

All of the living beings in the universe. This concept is contrasted with *bhajana*, the world or environment in which those beings live.

Shakyamuni (565–486 B.C.).

Literally, "the sage of the Shakya clan." The founder of Buddhism. Born as a prince in the small kingdom of Kapilavastu in central India, he was given the name Siddhartha Gautama. At the age of twenty-nine, he left his family to seek the way of liberation. After six years of painful searching, he attained enlightenment and became the Buddha ("Awakened One"). After that, he taught people the Dharma he had discovered. He died at the age of eighty.

Shan-tao.

See "Zendo."

Shin Buddhism.

See "Jodo Shinshu."

Shingon.

An esoteric Japanese Buddhist school which was founded by Kukai (A.D. 774–835). The term *shingon* means *mantra*, a word or phrase which has mystic power.

Shinran (A.D. 1173–1262).

The founder of the Jodo Shinshu school. Born in Kyoto as a son of Hino Arinori, an aristocrat. In 1181, he became a monk on Mt. Hiei, where he was trained in Tendai teachings and practice for ten years. In 1191 he traveled to Kofukuji Temple in Nara to study. In 1197 he returned to Mt. Hiei, where he was in charge of a meditation hall. In 1201 he attempted to meditate in the Rokkakudo Hall for one hundred days. On the ninety-fifth day he had a vision of Prince Shotoku. After that, he visited Honen (1133–1212), the founder of the Jodo school, at Yoshimizu. Deeply impressed by Honen, he became his follower and started to practice the Nembutsu exclusively. Honen gave him the name "Shakku." When he was thirty, he again changed his name, to Zenshin, after the Bodhisattva Avalokitesvara called him by that name in a dream. In 1207, because of official persecution of the Nembutsu movement, he was exiled to Kokufu in Echigo (the present Niigata

172

Prefecture), deprived of his priestly status, and given a lay name, Fujii Yoshizane. In Echigo he married Eshinni, had children, and gave himself yet another name, Gutoku Shinran ("Foolish Bald-Headed Shinran"). In 1211 he was pardoned, but did not return to Kyoto. In 1214 he moved to the Kanto area (the present Tokyo area), where he taught the Nembutsu. In 1224 he composed his main work, the *Kyogyoshinsho*, at Inada. When he was around sixty years old, after staying in Hitachi for about twenty years, he returned to Kyoto. There he composed a number of texts, including many *wasan* (Japanese Buddhist hymns). In 1256 he disowned his oldest son Zenran for having deceived the Nembutsu followers in the Kanto area by claiming, falsely, that his father had transmitted a secret teaching to him. The resulting confusion moved some of Shinran's disciples to visit him in Kyoto and inquire into his views on Buddhism. Yuien-bo, the author of the *Tannisho*, was one of those visitors.

Shinshu ("True Teaching [or School]").
An abridged form of "Jodo Shinshu." *See* "Jodo Shinshu."

Shonin.
An honorific title used for the founder of a Buddhist school or for an eminent monk. Examples: Shinran Shonin and Honen Shonin.

Shotoku Taishi (or Prince Shotoku, A.D. 574–622).
An ancient ruler who was one of the earliest patrons of Buddhism in Japan. He wrote commentaries on three Mahayana sutras: the *Lotus Sutra*, the *Vimalakirti-nirdesa-sutra*, and the *Srimaladevi-simhanada-sutra*. (*T.* vol. 56, pp. 1–127.) In 604, he promulgated the first Japanese constitution, the Seventeen-Article Constitution, which was based on Buddhist and Confucian ideals.

Six Realms of Mortal Existence (or Six Paths).
1) the realm of the gods, 2) the realm of humans, 3) the realm of fighting demons, 4) the realm of animals, 5) the realm of hungry ghosts, and 6) hell. All beings transmigrate through these realms in accordance with their karma. Those who commit grave sins fall into hell, where they are tortured for a very long time, though not eternally, as punishment for their sins. *See* "Samsara."

Six Sense Organs.
> The eye, ear, nose, tongue, body, and mind.

Suchness (Skt. *tathata*).
> *See* "Truth of Non-Origination."

Supernatural Abilities (Skt. *abhijna*).
> The supernatural powers of Buddhas and Bodhisattvas. They are: 1) the ability to manifest oneself in any place, 2) the ability to see things at any distance, 3) the ability to hear any sound at any distance, 4) the ability to know the thoughts of others, 5) the ability to know the past lives of oneself and others, and 6) the power to totally eradicate defilements.

Sutra.
> Those Buddhist scriptures which contain the sermons of the Buddha. One of the three categories of Buddhist literature, which are known as the three baskets (*tripitaka*).

Tathagata.
> One of the ten epithets of the Buddha. It means "one who has gone to (*gata*) and come from (*agata*) the truth of suchness (*tatha*)," i.e., "one who embodies the truth of suchness (*tatha*)." In Pure Land Buddhism it refers to either Amida Buddha or Shakyamuni Buddha.

Ten Evil Deeds.
> 1) Killing, 2) stealing, 3) sexual misconduct, 4) lying, 5) uttering harsh words, 6) uttering words which cause division, 7) frivolous talk, 8) greed, 9) anger, and 10) holding wrong views.

Ten Quarters.
> The eight points of the compass, plus the zenith and the nadir. The expression "in the ten quarters" means "everywhere in the universe."

Tendai (Ch. T'ien-t'ai).
> This Mahayana school was founded in China by Chigi (Chih-i, 538–97) and was based on the *Lotus Sutra* and the doctrines of Nagarjuna. Japanese Tendai was established when Saicho brought the Tendai tradition back from China in 805. Later he built the Enryakuji temple on Mt. Hiei as a center of the study and practice of Tendai. Japanese Tendai differs from Chinese Tendai in that it is a doctrinal system consisting of a mixture of

Chinese Tendai, Zen, esoteric teachings, and Mahayana precepts. *See* "Mt. Hiei," "Shinran," *and* "Honen."

Theravada ("The School of the Elders").
The sole survivor of the eighteen Hinayana schools. It is the dominant school in Sri Lanka, Burma, Thailand, Cambodia, and Laos.

Things-As-They-Really-Are.
See "Truth of Non-Origination."

Thirty-two Major Marks (of a Buddha).
The thirty-two excellent physical marks of a Buddha.

Three Mystic Practices.
1) Bodily mystic practice (mudra), meaning bodily (or manual) expressions of mystic signs, 2) verbal mystic practice (mantra), meaning the recitation of magical words, and 3) mental mystic practice (samadhi), meaning meditation on a Buddha or Bodhisattva. When the three mystic practices of a Buddha and those of a practitioner become united, the practitioner realizes Buddhahood in this life.

Three Worlds.
The three realms in which sentient beings transmigrate. They are:
1) The world of desire, which consists of the six realms of mortal existence. Sentient beings in this world possess lust, greed, hatred, jealousy, and other passions. *See* "Six Realms of Mortal Existence."
2) The world of form, which consists of sixteen heavens in which all material things are beautiful. Beings in this world have neither sexual desire nor appetites.
3) The world of non-form, which consists of four heavens in which no material things exist. Beings in this world enjoy deep meditation.

Transformed (Buddha) Body.
The third of the three bodies of the Buddha (*trikaya*). They are:
1) Dharma-Body (Skt. *dharma-kaya*), "the ultimate truth," which is formless, indescribable, and inconceivable. It is the same thing as the truth of non-origination or suchness.
2) Body of Recompense (*sambhoga-kaya*), a symbolic personification of the Dharma-body. The word "recompense"

means that it is a Buddha-body which was realized as a "recompense (or reward)" for the vows and practice of a Bodhisattva. This Buddha-body always resides in the Pure Land. Example: Amida Buddha.

3) Transformed Body (Skt. *nirmana-kaya*), an "incarnate" or "historically manifested" body of a Buddha which appears in the world to guide sentient beings in a manner adapted to their situations and abilities. Example: Shakyamuni Buddha.

Transformed Land.
The third of the following three Buddha Lands:
1) True (Buddha) Land, the land of ultimate truth.
2) (Buddha) Land of Recompense, where Nembutsu practitioners with true faith are born.
3) Transformed (Buddha) Land, where Nembutsu practitioners who doubt Other Power are born.

True Land of Recompense.
See "Land of Recompense."

Truth of Non-Origination.
The first half of "Neither originating nor perishing," a phrase often used by Mahayanists to describe the ultimate nature of things. This phrase means that although phenomena appear to originate and perish, when they are seen from the viewpoint of ultimate reality, they do not. This truth is also called "Dharma-nature," "things-as-they-really-are," or "suchness."

Transmigration.
See "Samsara."

Utmost Bliss (Skt. *Sukhavati*, "possessing bliss").
The name of the Buddha Land in the Western quarter which the Bodhisattva Dharmakara created when he became Amida Buddha. This land symbolizes the sphere of ultimate truth (Dharma), or of perfect peace and happiness. In the Sino-Japanese Buddhist tradition it came to be identified with "the Pure Land (*Jodo*)."

Vasubandhu (Jpn. Seshin or Tenjin, ca. A.D. 300–400).
The second of the seven patriarchs of Jodo Shinshu, and the author of Abhidharma and Yogacara texts. His *Pure Land*

Treatise (*T.* vol. 26, pp. 230–3), a commentary on the *Larger Sukhavativyuha-sutra*, became one of the basic texts of the Pure Land tradition in China and Japan. *See* "Donran."

Vow (Skt. *pranidhana*).

At the outset of his practice, a Bodhisattva makes vows to attain enlightenment. *See* "Original Vow" *and* "Four Vows of a Bodhisattva."

Wasan.

A Japanese Buddhist hymn which praises the virtues of a Buddha, Bodhisattva, or patriarch. Shinran composed three collections of *wasans* (*T.* vol. 83, pp. 655–69): 1) *Jodo Wasan* (Hymns in Praise of the Pure Land); 2) *Koso Wasan* (Hymns in Praise of the Patriarchs); and 3) *Shozomatsu Wasan* (Hymns about the True Dharma [Period], the Image Dharma [Period], and the Final Dharma [Period]).

Wisdom (Skt. *prajna*).

Wisdom and compassion are the two most important virtues in Mahayana Buddhism. A Buddha is one who has perfected these two virtues.

Womb Palace.

The part of the Pure Land where those of imperfect faith are reborn inside lotus buds. There they remain shut up for several kalpas and can neither see the Buddha nor hear his teaching. Eventually, however, the lotus buds open and they attain enlightenment.

Yuien-bo (A.D. 1223–90).

Originally from the Hitachi Province, his lay name was Heijiro. After becoming a disciple of Shinran, he built a temple at Kawada in Ibaragi Province. About thirty years after Shinran's death, he wrote the *Tannisho.*

Yuishinsho ("By Faith Alone") (*T.* vol. 93, pp. 910–5).

A text written by Seikaku (A.D. 1166–1235), a disciple of Honen. Shinran wrote a commentary on this text entitled *Yuishinsho Mon'i* ("The Essentials of *By Faith Alone*") (*T.* vol. 93, pp. 699–704).

Zazen ("Sitting Meditation").

The chief practice of the Zen school.

Zendo (Shan-tao, A.D. 613–81).

> The fifth of the seven patriarchs of the Jodo Shinshu. He is known as the systematizer of Chinese Pure Land doctrine. His principle work is his *Commentary on the Meditation Sutra* (*T.* vol. 37, pp. 245–78), which is in four volumes. Honen became a Pure Land follower after reading this text. *See* "Honen."

Zenran (A. D. 1212–92).

> Shinran's oldest son. *See* "Shinran."

Zenshin.

> One of Shinran's names. *See* "Shinran."

Bibliography

In Japanese (Original)

Shinran Shonin Zenshu. Vol. of "Genko-hen." Tokyo: Shinran Shonin Zenshu Kankokai, 1959, 1–42.

Shinshu Shogyo Zensho. Vol. II. Kyoto: Kokyoshoin, 1958, 773–95.

Taisho Shinshu Daizokyo. Edited by Taisho Shinshu Daizokyo Kankokai. Vol. 83, No. 2661. Tokyo: Daizo Shuppan, 1931, 728–35.

In English

[Yuien-bo]. *The Tannisho, Tract on Deploring the Heterodoxies: An Important Textbook of Shin Buddhism Founded by Shinran (1173–1262).* Translated by Tosui Imadate. Kyoto: The Eastern Buddhist Society, 1928, 1939.

—————. *The Tannisho: A Religion Beyond Good and Evil.* Translated by Ryukyo Fujimoto. Kyoto: Honpa Hongwanji, 1932, 1955.

—————. *Shinran-Shonin's Tannisho with Buddhist Psalms.* Translated by Saizo Inagaki. Toyonaka: Eishinsha, 1949.

—————. "The Tannisho by Yuien." Translated by Kosho Yamamoto. In *Shinshu Seiten,* 263–81. Honolulu: Honpa Hongwanji Mission of Hawaii, 1955.

—————. *Tannisho.* Translated by Asoka Society. San Francisco: Asoka Society, 1961.

—————. *Tannisho: A Tract Deploring the Heterodoxies of Faith.* Translated by Kosho Otani et al. Kyoto: Higashi Honganji, 1961.

—————. *The Tanni Sho: Notes Lamenting Differences.* Translated by Ryosetsu Fujiwara. Ryukoku Translation Series, No. II. Kyoto: Ryukoku University, 1962.

—————. "The Tannisho." Translated by D. T. Suzuki. In D. T. Suzuki. *Collected Works on Shin Buddhism,* 190–222. Kyoto: Shinshu Otaniha, 1973.

_____ . *Tannisho: Lamenting the Deviations.* Translated by Taitetsu Unno. Honolulu: Buddhist Study Center, 1977.

_____ . "Notes Lamenting Differences." In *Shinshu Seiten: Jodo Shin Buddhist Teaching*, 250–68. San Francisco: Buddhist Churches of America, 1978.

_____ . *Tannisho: Passages Deploring Deviations of Faith.* Translated by Shojun Bando and Harold Stewart. Kyoto: The Eastern Buddhist Society, 1980.

_____ . *Tannisho: A Primer.* Translated by Dennis Hirota. Kyoto: Ryukoku University, 1982.

_____ . *Tannisho: A Shin Buddhist Classic.* Translated by Taitetsu Unno. Honolulu: Buddhist Study Center, 1984.

In French

[Yuien-bo]. "*Tannisyo*, regret de la croyance etrangere." Translated by Nyoiti Sakurazawa. In *Principe unique de la philosophie et de la science d'Extreme-Orient*, 125–55. Paris: Libraire Philosophique J. Vrin, 1968.

_____ . *Tanni-Sho: sur le regret de l'alteration de la vraie croyance.* Translated by Osamu Yamada. Geneve: Societe Bouddhique Suisse Jodo-Shin, 1971.

_____ . *Tannisho: notes deplorant les divergences.* Translated by Jerome Ducor. Kyoto: International Association of Buddhist Culture, 1983.

In German

[Yuien-bo]. *Tan-i-sho: Amida Unsere Zuflucht, Urkunden zum Verständnis des Japanischen Sukhavati-Buddhismus.* Translated by Hans Haas. In *Quellen der Religions Geschichte*, Vol. 2. Gottingen: Vandenhöch & Ruprecht, 1910.

_____ . *Tannisho: das Buchlein vom Bedauern des abweichenden Glaubens.* Translated by Eikichi Ikeyama. 2nd ed. Kyoto: Hozokan, 1940.

_____ . *Tannisho: das Buchlein vom Bedauern des abweichenden Glaubens.* Translated by Michio Sato. Kyoto: Honpa Honganji, 1977.

_____ . *Tannisho: die Gunst des reinen Landes.* Translated by Ryogi Okochi and Klaus Otte. Bern: Origo Verlag, 1979.

In Korean

[Yuien-bo]. *Tannisho kaisetsu: Shinko no seizui.* Translated by Ri Chiko. Seoul: Chosen Jikei Kyokai, 1928.

In Portuguese

[Yuien-bo]. *Tannisho: O Tratado de Lamentacao das Heresias.* Translated by Professor Ricardo Mario Goncalves. Sao Paulo: Templo Budista Higashi-Honganji, 1974.

In Tibetan

[Yuien-bo]. *Tannisho.* Translated by Kaiun Shiratate. In *Kenkyusho Kiyo*, No. 6, 1–58. Kyoto: Otani Daigaku Shinshu Sogo Kenkyujo, 1988.

Index